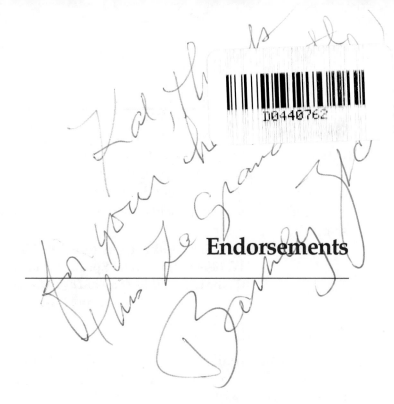

Endorsements

"There is a lot of information in today's world but not an abundance of wisdom. Bernard Hale Zick's *The Negotiating Paradox* is loaded with insight, enlightenment, and knowledge about one of the most important topics in American business. I have benefited from it . . . you will too!"

Scott McKain, CSP, CPAE;
President, McKain Performance Group.
All Business Is Show Business.

"We all continuously negotiate—whether we know it or not. There are dozens of tips in Barney's book that we can immediately use."

Bert Decker, CSP, CPAE;
You've Got To Be Believed To Be Heard.

"Here at Walters International Speakers Bureau we have long known Barney Zick as the Consummate Negotiator. Barney is indeed the ultimate "Friendly Persuader." How tremendous to have all of his brilliant secrets in one book. *The Negotiating Paradox: How You Can Get More by Giving More* is so good you should buy one for every sales person on your staff—then watch your sales soar!"

Dottie Walters, CSP; *Speak & Grow Rich;* **President, Walters International Speakers Bureau; Publisher,** S*haring Ideas Magazine for Professional Speakers.*

"Barney really sets the record straight as negotiating as a giving process! Thanks Barney. Everyone must read."

Thomas J. Winninger, CSP, CPAE; Founder Winninger Institute; *Price Wars: Sell Easy: Hiring Smart.*

"I was on my way to a meeting when I picked up a copy of Barney's manuscript, thinking I would just glance it over. I found myself engrossed in immediately useful information on negotiating tactics, written in a simple, easy-to-read style. Wow! Great work, Barney."

Bobbie Gee, CSP, CPAE, Speaker Hall of Fame.

"What a revolutionary new way to build your business. It's a must read."

Scott Friedman, CSP; Motivational Humorist; *Using Humor for a Change.*

"Barney Zick can show you how generosity pays! To get more, give more...to have more, help more. These are ideas I express and embrace in *The Acorn Principle*. Now Barney shows you how to apply them in business dealings. In fact, here's another: To win more...read this book!"
Jim Cathcart, CSP, CPAE; Founder & CEO Cathcart Institute, La Jolla, CA.

"Bernard's book on negotiating is a breath of fresh air. Finally someone has written on the subject of negotiating recognizing the importance of developing and maintaining win-win, positive, and long-term relationships. Congratulations, Bernard, on a superb book."
Tim Connor, CSP–Best Selling Author and Speaker of *Soft Sell & The Road to Happiness Is Full of Potholes.*

"At last! A book with heart about Negotiation. Barney Zick offers a new slant on a tough subject."
David Yoho, Jr. CPAE, Speaker Hall of Fame; President, Professional Educators, Inc.

"Excellent techniques you can use to negotiate better."
Randy Gage; President, Gage Direct Marketing.

"Barney Zick provides invaluable insights, strategies, and techniques for winning the negotiation game."
Paul Karasik, *Sweet Persuasion.* *How to Make It Big in the Seminar Business.*

The Negotiating Paradox

How You Can Get More by Giving More

Bernard Zick

Skyward Publishing
Dallas, Texas

Copyright 2000 by Skyward Publishing, Inc.

Publisher: Skyward Publishing, Inc
               17440 North Dallas Parkway
               Suite 100
               Dallas, Texas 75287
               Phone/Fax (573) 717-1040
               E-Mail: skyward@sheltonbbs.com
               Website: www.skywardpublishing.com

Library of Congress Cataloging-in-Publication Data

Zick, Bernard
        The negotiating paradox: how you can get more / by giving
more
Bernard Hale Zick.
        p.   cm.
        ISBN 1-881554-00-7
        1. Negotiation in business   I. Title.
HD58.6.Z53   2000
658.4'052--dc21

                                        99-29258
                                        CIP

Acknowledgments

It has been more than a decade since I joined forces with Douglas E. Gilliss, J.D., to explore the subject of negotiating. Because he is an attorney and a college professor, Doug's focus, by acquired nature, is in structure. He is responsible for the development of our three-step model known as "The Target Negotiating System." My role was to incorporate the practical experiences and powerful phrases into the mix. Doug has been an invaluable team player to whom I owe much, not only for this book but also in so many other ways as well.

Legal lessons and experiences of this book and my entire career were also acquired from my stepfather and from my former wife. After forty years of living with lawyers, one naturally picks up a little of the legal aspects of deal making. Thanks.

MacRae "Mac" Ross has been my mentor in business for fifteen years. He has taught me to look beyond what is on paper to what people will actually *do* in any given situation.

Major contributors of ideas, edits, and additions to the book were my good friends, Jim Harris and Doug Gilliss.

But, without a doubt, the best and toughest

negotiators I have ever faced have been my children, Robert, Andy, Derek and Katrina. I only wish that I could be as inventive and persistent in my negotiations as they always have been in their negotiating bouts with me. I would win every time.

This book is dedicated to Douglas E. Gilliss, my partner for over a decade, who aided in discovering negotiating principles and is and the originator of the "Target Negotiating System," to Jim Harris for his unending help on this book, and to my children, Robert, Andrew, Derek and Katrina, the toughest negotiators I have ever faced!

Contents

Introduction
Meet the Friendly Persuader

Professional football has its All-Pros. The insurance industry has its CLUs. Accounting has its CPAs. Even auto mechanics can be "Certified." Now, there is something here for you, the negotiator. By the time you complete this book, you will have acquired the methods and techniques used by the most highly successful business people and professionals as they negotiate their way through life. You will have attained the highest status of negotiation. You will have achieved the status of a "Friendly Persuader."

Think that sounds too wimpy? Perhaps you expected something more macho like "Super Negotiator" or "All-American Arm Twister." No! This is part of the overall strategy behind *The Negotiating Paradox*. You want to become exactly the opposite of what your negotiating counterpart expects you to be. The shock alone can be a form of strength.

Often in negotiation seminars, trainers tell us that to get what we want in today's dog-eat-dog world, we have to negotiate fiercely and use tricks, wit, and pressure. I highly disagree. In fact, I have discovered a negotiating paradox. *You can actually get more by giving more.* My system will give you the competitive edge in the office, the home, or wherever you interact with others. Learning it is simple and easy. Let us dismiss the myth that some people are born negotiators. We do realize that some people seem to have natural-born talents. It is also true that some people pick up skills faster or seem to apply them better than others. However, with or without these natural talents or abilities, you *can*, with a small helping of acquired knowledge and a little bit of practice, negotiate better. The more skillful you are at negotiating, the easier it will be for you to find alternative solutions to every problem, no matter how large or how small it may be. It is a creative, problem-solving way to think—and to negotiate.

Many of you have picked up this book because you quickly and easily recognize you are in a business or profession where negotiation isn't just a watchword but is a way of life. If you're an attorney, real-estate broker, business or financial consultant, salesperson, marketing specialist, or any similar professional, this book is a natural for you.

But, this book is for everyone else, as well. Probably without realizing it you were involved in some kind of negotiation today, or yesterday, or you will be tomorrow. Whatever your role, profession, or status in life, you are consumed with the process of *getting along* from day to day, and getting along from day to day centers around negotiations in one form or another. When you interact with the hostess who seats you at a restaurant, or when you communicate with your customers, co-workers, or your boss, you are negotiating. When you try to get a parking space ahead of someone else or shop for a shirt or a new set of tires, you are negotiating. Negotiation goes beyond your interactions at work. Everyday exchanges are forms of negotiation.

Regardless of who you are or what you do for a living, there is something in this book for you. In fact, the concepts learned will reap many times your investment in time, to say nothing of the price of the book. You see, though few may realize it, the ability to negotiate well is an acquired skill, and the more skills you have, and the more adept you are at using them, the better you will be able to get along in life. Like the proverbial example of learning to ride a bicycle, first you master certain principles and rules, and then you practice, practice, practice.

Eventually this acquired skill becomes a part of your persona—you never forget it. Even those of us who haven't been on a bicycle for years could still mount and ride—perhaps a bit wobbly—but without falling. Even so, how comfortable would we be? Think of that tiny seat! Now, imagine yourself at the starting line as a contestant in the *Tour de France*. Ridiculous? Of course. The difference is conditioning and training.

We've all lived with the old adage: *practice makes perfect*. Well, I hate to burst a myth, but that saying just isn't true. If your practice is inappropriate, your performance will be incorrect. Perfect practice makes perfect performance. If your goal is to do more than just *get by*, you must do more than learn the basic rules and skills of negotiation. If you want optimum results, go beyond the norm. The ideas taught in this book will substantially help you to develop your negotiation skills , and those skills will help you climb the ladder of success.

The concepts taught in The *Negotiating Paradox* make it easy to learn effective negotiation skills. To simplify the process, the methods I use here are broken into five areas of focus:

> *Know your desired outcomes.*

> *Know your client.*

> *Know what makes you unique.*

> *Ask for more than you want.*

> *Play the trading game.*

These steps are simple and easy to master, and once you master them, you'll be glad you did.

It is important that you settle in with the constant reminder that by reading this book you are going to become a Friendly Persuader, a person who negotiates calmly and stays in control. To help acclimate yourself to your soon-to-be-acquired status, you should picture yourself each time you encounter the term, Friendly Persuader, throughout this book. The person behind that name is always going to be you.

Another term you will frequently encounter here is a reference to the person with whom you are interacting in a negotiation. This could be your barber or hair stylist, an opposing attorney, a merger candidate, a clothing-store clerk, an IRS agent, or your mother-in-law. In any event or situation, begin thinking of the person you are interacting with as your Negotiation Nemesis—not an enemy, just a worthy opponent.

As a Friendly Persuader, you are out to get more of what you want. You can also be assured that your

Negotiating Nemesis is out to do the same. Thus, the plot is set for this book. Plenty of action and conflict will hold your attention as you encounter problems and solutions. It may make you chuckle over a fond memory or mentally kick yourself in the hindside, but mostly it will make you think and act like a winner. If you weave *The Negotiating Paradox* principles and techniques into your everyday life, you'll get the best of all that is good in life, and you'll do so in a disarmingly friendly manner that is calmly and forcefully persuasive. Yes, you've seen others get what they want by acting that way, and now you can do it, too.

Come on. Let's discover how to *give more to get more.* There is a Friendly Persuader inside you screaming to be set free.

1

You Must Play in Order to Win

The world's largest publisher of business and self-help programs on audio cassette tapes recently asked me to speak at a conference in London. I had labored long and hard for this assignment and was excited that I had been selected to attend as a guest lecturer. I had really wanted to attend and participate in one of his conferences for a long time. But, I have always maintained that *"want-ers"* — those who really, really *want* something — make bad negotiators.

When a lady from the company called to address the amount of my speaking fee, I was anxious to defuse the conversation and conclude the contract discussion. I quickly told the convention manager how excited and honored I was to have been chosen to participate and proclaimed in my toughest negotiating manner, "Whatever you're offering, I'm sure, will be fine."

I'm certain that really took her off guard. When she finally began to address the speaking fee, it was really quite low, but remember, I wanted this engagement.

To move toward closure, I said, "I'm sure we can work things out. Tell me the rest of the deal, and we'll get back to the fee." (Notice that money was moved to the end of the discussion so that all other terms and conditions were put on the table first.)

She described several perks including a hotel suite for a week and other amenities that were actually quite pleasing. Now remember, I wanted this trip and not just to see London one more time. Additional business, more valuable than a dozen speaking fees, could be generated from the three-day conference. Having decided against playing hard ball, I was charming and easy to work with, but I didn't want to leave money on the table either. Since she was booking me to speak on the subject of "Negotiation Techniques" she was obviously familiar with my background and experience in negotiating. Therefore, it was more than likely that she was holding back part of the fee as a negotiating ploy.

"Sounds fine," I said. "As I told you earlier, I really do want to go, so I won't even negotiate with you. But, before we complete this deal, let me ask you a question. Am I correct in assuming that you started with a low offer knowing that I would automatically ask for more?"

A reluctant "Yes" came through with a smile that crossed telephone lines and the expanse of the Atlantic Ocean.

"Then, since we both know that there is an extra amount that you were already prepared to offer, I won't even ask what it is. Why don't you just include that extra amount in our agreement, and I'll sign whatever you send over to me." How much gentler could an offer be? And, the extra amount that she sent was enough to pay for another first-class airfare to London.

Such is the game being played every day, and this

game has an unusual set of rules. You've been tossed into the game, and no one even bothered to tell you. As a participant, you either play and win, or alternatively, avoid playing, and you lose. The name of this game, *negotiation*, like any other game, is best played by following the rules.

You Must Negotiate

For those unfamiliar with negotiation skills, the term *negotiation* is generally reserved for the isolated occasions when they haggle over price when purchasing large items such as a house or a car. Otherwise, they are prone to mentally exclude themselves from participating in negotiations. With these assumptions, the term is linked only to those of higher ranking powers such as the Secretary of State or diplomats of the United Nations.

With worldwide media attention, such officials do negotiate to resolve a world crisis, but these public officials are not the only ones who negotiate. We all do. Even if we are unaware of negotiation concepts, the fact is, we all negotiate in some fashion daily. Therefore, consciously bringing negotiation theories within the parameters of our daily thinking moves us to higher levels of awareness and ultimately to success.

In outdated training seminars that have emerged over recent years, a trainer typically recounts a myriad of case studies where Henry Kissinger averted an international crisis in volatile Central America, South Africa, the Middle East, or some other political hot spot. We are supposed to be appropriately "wowed." The speaker then treats us to a series of tactical ploys that are comparable to chess moves. We are told that the use of these tactics, called *gambits*, will assuredly bring quick settlements favorable to us. In bringing the talk to an end, the speaker inevitably encourages attendees to use the ever popular *win-win* strategy. This technique, by design, forces us to compromise in order to avoid the strong-arm tactics sure to be used by our counterpart.

I'm telling you that you should approach the *win-win* strategy with caution. In fact, I'll go so far as to state that you should *not* use it. I believe it to be a weak procedure that costs in the end. When approached with queries, this traditional expert spares the audience's concerns and discloses the secrets of victory, thus leaving him or her available to speak another day. There is a better way.

Undoubtedly, some value exists in extracting universal principles from international negotiation strategies. However, it is unlikely these complicated procedures will enable you to save $100 off your next suit purchase, $1000 off your next new car, or successfully close a major deal with a customer. More effective negotiation skills, however, when applied to your own day-to-day encounters, will make a meaningful difference.

My goal in writing this book is to provide you with the basic negotiation skills that will help you prosper daily. Whether a marketing specialist, a homemaker, a clerk, or a career diplomat facing a demanding international incident, these sound and proven principles will work better for you than any learn-by-being-impressed approach or any guess-how-they-did-it method of learning. This innovative step-by-step method will increase your negotiation powers without limit. Equally as important, these strategies are actually fun to use.

Dealing with Others Is Negotiation

If we were to take the word *negotiation* and play a negotiation word-association game, we could undoubtedly make many connections such as *mediation*, a*ttorneys, arguments*, and *buying* (or *selling*). While these associations are appropriate, negotiation involves more. The main point to remember is that every day, all day long, without thinking about it, we negotiate. Whether buying or selling an item or service for household use, personal consumption, a business product or a professional service, we are negotiating.

Negotiation doesn't necessarily mean you ask for extra goods or services or seek a lower price. Negotiation is simply the act of dealing with others. The steps and strategies you utilize to present your wants or needs and the limits you place on what you in return will accept involves the negotiation process. This is true even if you are unaware of it.   Except for the most important business deals or large purchases, we typically spend little, if any, time in planning our purchases. We deal with people on a situational basis, aiming at getting our wants and needs met. With little thought, we use those personal interaction skills that we think will work.   We act tough in some situations and are easygoing in others.   Our behavior does not follow any set pattern, system, or model. With such a haphazard method, there is little consistency and frequently no predictability in how we execute our endeavors.

If anything is foreseen, it could be our all too eager compliance with the requests of others. Too often someone will simply say, "Sit here, pay this price, do this extra work, accept this quality, follow this procedure," and we do it. It is all to easy for us to just assume that organizations, agencies, or other people control our lives, and we passively accept that control in order to avert responsibility for making decisions. No wonder we are less than satisfied with life. My hope is that as you read this book you will change your attitude and perception. I hope to modify the very way you think. Learning to use effective negotiation strategies teaches you how to regain control of your life. The earned benefits will point you to new avenues of success.

Before moving on, let's momentarily summarize a few main points which will help us to mentally program our thought processes.

➤ *Negotiation is for everyday affairs.*

➤ *Negotiation is for important business deals.*

➤ *Negotiation enables people to exchange goods and services.*

➤ *Effective negotiation leaves both parties satisfied.*

➤ *Without negotiation, you'll receive less from life than you deserve.*

If you desire to know more about changing your life, read on.

Learn to Negotiate Every Day

I'm writing part of this book while sitting on a plane. My assigned seat, 4A, is a window seat in the last row of first class. Now, we all know that any seat in first class is better than the best seat in coach, but this particular seat, 4A, is probably my least favorite in first class. This seat doesn't recline fully due to the partition between the first class and coach section. Also, there is never enough elbow-room for someone of my size in a window seat.

Instead of taking my assigned seat upon boarding, I observed that there were several empty seats in first class, so I returned to the boarding gate. I asked the ticket agent if I could have seat 2E, which I had noted was vacant. Since 2E is the first aisle seat behind the galley, there is plenty of leg room, and it is, consequently, my favorite seat on an airplane. (At 6' 4", I need all the leg room I can get.)

The agent told me that my coveted 2E was reserved, although it hadn't been filled. She said that I might, of course, sit in it for the flight if the rightful occupant didn't board. I waltzed back onto the plane and sat in 2E.

To my delight, the drinks had been served, empty glasses collected, and our plane was pushing from the gate. I started pulling out all my stuff, reveling in the fact that I had won my prize seat.

Suddenly, the plane jolted and slowly moved back toward the gate which, as we all know, is an unusual procedure.

Two people, who appeared to be in their late twenties or early thirties, breathlessly rushed into the cabin. The young man looked straight at me and sternly said, "That's my seat."

Proudly, I straightened my shoulders. You see, I had started my negotiation planning for this seat long ago, and Ol' Barney was well prepared. Clearly, when I attempted to persuade the boarding agent to change

my seating arrangements, I knew I had someone else's
seat, so I had mentally formulated my plan and was
ready to put it into action. My plan was simple. I would
offer the seat next to me as an alternative. However, if
my Nemesis showed no interest in negotiating, I was
more than willing to give in without the slightest bit of
resistance since, after all, it *was* his assigned seat, and I
was the poacher.

Pointing to the window seat beside me, I stated,
"There's a vacant seat next to me that has just as much
leg room." (Short and sweet. This was my entire
negotiating script. The next move was his.)

He stated his reproach, "Well, you'll just have to
put up with me sitting next to you." He then slammed
himself into the seat. His comment made no sense, but
I didn't care. I had won almost by default. I had my
seat and assumed he would calm down and forget it
when we were in the air.

The plane departed, but before it reached cruising
level, the young man rang the flight attendant button.
Fearing an emergency, the attendant carefully worked
her way through the aisle to our row. The man then
asked the flight attendant if she could help with his
seating arrangements. His next words shocked me:
"I'm on my honeymoon."

Ol' Barney was deflated. The young man had to say
no more. I was totally embarrassed and immediately
eased from my seat without so much as a word, except
a mumbled apology to the young man and the flight
attendant. As much as I like to be comfortable while
flying, I refuse to stand in the way of true love.

The young man, though appearing to have
common sense, apparently was inept at negotiation. In
this case, he could have easily stood up for himself.

Without even a mention of words such as "newlywed" or "honeymoon," I would have moved had he merely said, "But I prefer that seat," or any such comment.

Neither he nor his silent bride had made it clear they were together. In fact, when the man sat next to me, the lady brusquely passed without speaking a word.

Don't you see people like that everyday? They let anger control emotions. When anger enters the picture, solutions to problems are stifled. When your thought processes are consumed with anger, your brain is so busy with emotional energy that it has little strength left for sorting out issues or solving problems. Frustration overpowers logic.

Psychologists tell us that anger forces our bodies to produce large amounts of hormones and that those hormones, if pumped excessively, will practically shut down our ability to think logically. Effective negotiators, therefore, deal with situations as they arise and avoid letting repressed emotions interfere with their ability to negotiate in a productive manner. They know that failing to do so actually winds up costing them in the negotiation.

Instead of letting anger override emotions, you should strive to keep your attention on issues or problems and concentrate on how you can solve them.

What Can We Learn?

Let's look at the lesson. So often in everyday business transactions, you encounter people who are ready to negotiate. If you fail to realize their ploys, you lose. Such people start out a little higher on their asking price or request a little more than they normally would and then wait for your move. If you fail to negotiate and do nothing (a frequent response), you lose.

Remember the young man with his new bride on the airplane? He lost heavily. Throughout the entire trip, his bride, now seated in my beloved and much coveted "2E," chewed him out. Her head jerked. Her finger waved, pointing at him for the entire flight. Good luck with that marriage. Had the poor guy simply asked me to move, he could have easily secured his seat with his bride next to him. Then, perhaps they might have smiled and held hands the entire trip, instead of . . . .

The Negotiation Game

The point is simple. Right after birth, you are rapidly launched into the game of life. As you mature, the game gains momentum and complexity. Through a constant series of negotiations, the game spins around you. Those aware of what is taking place learn to play. Those who don't, lose.

Whether you like it or not, you negotiate in some form or other, and you do so dozens of times daily. How can that be?

Some of you are thinking, "That statement may be true for others but not for me." Well, my friend, it is true for you. Be forewarned, and be prepared.

I submit that you are negotiating *even when you decide NOT to negotiate.* I contend that you are negotiating when you decide *not* to ask for more than you're offered, when you settle for less than you originally wanted or, worse still, when you permit others to dictate terms and conditions for you. On these terms, you have subconsciously decided to let the other person win. Let me prove this point.

Customer Service and Negotiation

The heart and soul of customer service is an employee negotiating with a customer. Customer service personnel who improperly handle customers or treat them with insensitivity damage potential relationship-enhancing opportunities. On my regular business visits to Seattle, I routinely booked rooms at the Marriott Hotel located just outside the entrance to the airport. Since I frequently arrived in Seattle late and needed to catch up on sleep before heading into the city the next morning for appointments, this nearby hotel best served my needs.

On one particular trip, my flight arrived earlier than usual. Ron Baker, a long-standing friend, picked me up at the airport, and we dined at the nearby Three Coins Restaurant. After a leisurely dinner and enjoyable visit, Ron drove up the hill to the Marriott. The time was approaching 11 p.m. Since we didn't want to unpack the car until we decided how close we were to my assigned room, we walked inside to check in with the clerk.

Presenting the young lady at the registration desk with a coupon that entitled me to a free room upgrade, I quietly waited for her reply. To my surprise, she firmly replied, "This coupon is not honored here."

"Is there a reason why?" I asked, withdrawing the coupon.

"Those are honored only at participating Marriott locations. Ours is not one of them." Her face was stern, and she clearly wanted me to melt away.

"Well, I regularly stay at Marriott Hotels," I calmly replied, although I was somewhat annoyed by her seeming indifference. "And, have for years had a

Marriott Marquee Gold Card," I added, assuming she would be more than obliged to accommodate me. Then, attaching one of my favorite lines, I cordially asked, "Is there anything extra you can do for me since you can't honor this coupon?"

I really wasn't looking for much, but I was negotiating for something. Anything? In fact, if she had said the hotel was "full to the gills" and all she could do was give me a pleasant smile and hope that I would take one of the few remaining rooms, I would have said, "That's good enough."

In fairness, I should point out here that I expect, and normally get, excellent service at Marriotts, so much so that they will always get a second chance from me. In fact, all I wanted was an acknowledgment that I was someone special, a Marriott Marquee Club Member and all-around nice guy. Don't most of us want someone to treat us a bit special? Sometimes even the least of efforts bring customer satisfaction.

Instead of a courteous reply, the young lady's firm tone again announced that my coupon was invalid and that there was absolutely nothing she could or would do.

What Could She Have Done?

I could have suggested a long list. She could have promised to give me two newspapers instead of one. She could have written me a note for a free cup of coffee in the morning, an act which would probably cost the hotel a whole 25 to 50 cents but would have insured that I ate breakfast there, allowing them a profit many times that amount. Actually, she could have done any of a dozen and one things. Since I was a little put off by her scornful nature, I said, "Thank you very much," and I walked out the door with my friend in tow. He asked, "What next?"

My Next Move

Once outside, I spotted a newly-built Holiday Inn at the bottom of the hill. I'm not an elitist, but considering the large number of nights I spend in hotel rooms each year, I have adopted the attitude that the more stars following the hotel name, the more comfortable I'll be, so I generally avoid Holiday Inns. Yet, this one looked to be quite promising, and I had been treated poorly at my favorite hotel. Not to mention that it was now, with the time difference, approaching 2 a.m. Briefly assessing the situation, I surmised that a new hotel had to be freshly decorated, so why not test it? I was certain of one thing. I wasn't staying in the Marriott.

The Holiday Inn room was spacious, comfortable, efficient, and cost a lot less than the Marriott. In fact, now the Holiday Inn is my first hotel preference in Seattle. If the Marriott clerk had realized that customer service is a matter of negotiation, I never would have discovered the alternative hotel. (Take note, hotel managers. This book should be assigned reading for hotel staff.)

People on the whole are easy to please. Most are agreeable if offered simple amenities that perhaps cost little or nothing. A kind word or a friendly smile keeps customers returning to you instead of searching for other places to take their business.

This example and many others prove time and again that basic negotiation skills allow you and your employees to do wonders on the job. Every employee you hire should know the simple principles taught in this book. This book could be the most profitable gift you ever give.

An Ounce of Negotiation

How many instances have there been when you could have, on behalf of yourself as an owner, or on behalf of your employer, done just one ounce of negotiating and made a situation much better? People like to believe that they are exempt from the rules. In the public sector, those are the very people who believe they can treat customers sternly or sourly without being censured. Perhaps that person can "get by with it" if the customer doesn't take time to complain to proper personnel, but that sour attitude often costs the company money.

When you exercise rules without a smile, you do disservice to customers and most often will offend a polished negotiator.

When to Negotiate?

Even day-to-day shopping revolves around negotiations. Last Christmas my oldest son, Robert, wanted a double bass drum pedal. Since he's been playing drums for a while, we own almost every piece of drum equipment available, except a bass pedal. This is a rather expensive item which can cost $300 or more. Robert, knowing that the pedal was expensive, thoughtfully suggested that we consider a used one and volunteered that he would consider it his Christmas present *and* his birthday present. That kid can already negotiate.

Because I'm prone to spend and can better justify money spent on sports equipment, musical instruments, and similar items with learning value attached to them, I am generally somewhat lenient. This request fit into the "exception to the rule" category. Other toys can and do wait.

After my son made a quick phone call to the store to confirm that the owner did have a pre-owned bass pedal in good condition for $260, I was ready to make the purchase. Mind you, I love to negotiate, but I'm not the kind of shopper who enjoys spending exorbitant amounts of time running from store to store searching for the best bargain.

This approach works against my ability to negotiate super deals because the amount of energy put into a negotiation must coincide with the additional benefit I might expect to receive. I'll be the first to openly admit that my weak shopping skills pale in the light of high-class shoppers, so I realize that I may not be in the best position to get a great deal. But, I did know the costs of used bass drum pedals. And, my hectic Christmas shopping schedule did not prevent me from staying true to my old adage: *Don't ever forget to negotiate.*

As the store owner talked, I looked at the used bass pedal, which was in like-new condition, except for a slight bit of discoloration on the part that contacts the drum. Great! The salesperson gave me the retail price for a similar bass drum pedal (which was phenomenal, and which I already knew) adding, "And, this set is only $260."

I confidently said, "But, surely you're willing to negotiate a little bit off that, aren't you?"

His millisecond reply was, "Yes, I can give it to you

for $225." This owner was obviously accustomed to negotiating and even expected his customers to negotiate.

I was pleased. Just because I remembered to ask, the price dropped, but since it dropped so readily, I wondered if I could make a better deal. I carefully examined the drum pedal, saying, "At that price, you're surely including the sales tax."

"Not possible," the owner said. "Drives the computer nuts if we don't collect sales tax, but tell you what I'll do. I'll let you have it for $200, and then we'll add the sales tax on top."

Well, we're not at 12 1/2% sales tax in Houston—at least not yet. The owner had, without cause, just handed over another major discount. In fact, if necessary, I would have gladly paid $225 plus the sales tax. Instead, I was paying $200 plus an additional $15 for sales tax, a savings of more than $60 from the original asking price. Sixty dollars will buy bundles of stocking stuffers for four kids and render untold hours of smugness and satisfaction for a negotiating Dad.

It Happens Every Day

This kind of situation happens repeatedly. The drum pedal purchase is just another example of a simple everyday negotiation. If I had thought the original price for a used piece of equipment was too high, I might have left the store and sought a bargain elsewhere. After going from store to store, I might have found another used drum pedal for less than $260, but maybe not. In any event that would have caused me to spend considerable time and effort running all over town, and it was getting late. Would I have saved more than $60? Probably not. The store owner, my Negotiating Nemesis, was satisfied with the deal. He is in the business of selling musical equipment. He made a sale. If I had ignored negotiating and had neither the time nor inclination to shop around, I would have lost $60. I prefer to win. Don't we all?

Negotiating for the Presidential Suite

Sometimes people have little knowledge of their negotiation abilities or opportunities because they mistakenly view themselves in inflexible positions when, in fact, a careful assessment of the situation would enable them to come up with some creative solutions. I remember an instance (prior to moving to Houston) when I was visiting that city to make a presentation at a convention for a large financial institution. Since I hadn't finalized my move to Houston, I eagerly accepted the chance to visit this enjoyable city again.

The convention was being held in a gorgeous hotel, The Westin Oaks in the Galleria area, which had a spacious and ornate lobby. I arrived in the city late in the evening and dragged into the hotel around 1 a.m. I knew that a room had been reserved for me and genuinely hoped and expected that my check-in at such a late hour wouldn't pose a problem. Was I ever wrong!

The very sweet and charming young woman at the reception desk softly said, "I'm sorry, but all our rooms are taken."

"But, what about my reservation? Barney Zick. Don't you have that name?" I asked tiredly, certain that she was mistaken and equally certain that she would discover the error of her ways by quickly and efficiently dispatching me to my reserved room. However, something deep inside me kept wondering if I was destined to sleep in the lobby.

"I'm sorry, Mr. Zick, but your name is not here and because of the convention, every room has been rented."

The clerk was pleasant enough, but her computer set the rules for who stayed in the hotel that night and who didn't. As far as her computer knew, I didn't exist. Mentally assessing the situation, I recognized my limited negotiating options. In this hotel, at this time, a very basic room with a view of the parking lot would rent for $125.

Having previously worked with the corporate sponsor who had handled the room arrangements, I knew the lowest priced rooms were assigned to speakers. The company's negotiated room rate was around $59, but I refused to let that fact diminish my stance. Why dwell on matters that talk you into a losing position?

Instead, I lightened the situation by jokingly asking the clerk if the hotel had spare pajamas I could borrow because, as I smilingly added, "It would be embarrassing to all of us for me to sleep in the lobby in the buff." We both laughed. My humor won her over. I was glad. I wanted to bring her over to my side of the issue. I wanted her to view me as the person who joked with her when there was a problem instead of the one who yelled and threw around threats or profanity.

Think about it this way. What do you think her reaction would have been if I had yelled at her? Would you rather be yelled at or joked with in such a situation? With a full hotel, she had to turn people away, and she undoubtedly had more than enough frustration for one day. She held an awkward position, the bearer of ill news to those with reservations but no room. She had no choice but to turn people away. In the hotel business, as in the airline industry, this dilemma is known as overbooking, and I can tell you it is unpleasant for anyone — guests who think a room awaits them, the management, and particularly the hapless young lady who at 1 a.m. has a frazzled, weary man leaning on her reception desk joking about sleeping in the lobby in the nude. At least she hoped he was joking. Despite it all, she had a pleasant smile.

Talking My Way into a Room

After a jovial conversation with the receptionist, I decided to make another move. "Are you absolutely certain that there isn't a single place with a door that hasn't been rented? I'll sleep on the conference table, if necessary."

She poked around in her computer. "The only unused room in the entire hotel is the Presidential Suite," she finally said.

Grinning from ear to ear, I slapped the counter and exclaimed, "That's it. That's the room meant for me. Perfect."

"Oh, I couldn't do that. That room rents for more than $1,800 per night."

I countered with my quasi-logic. "They told me in business school that you should always get permission whenever making a deviation from the rules. Have you been told that, too?"

She said, "Yes."

"And, if you can't get your supervisor to give you

permission, and you're still faced with a problem to solve, then it must be O.K. for you to make the decision. Isn't that right?"

She agreed, with a gleam in her eye.

"If you were to make the decision yourself, would you give me that room to sleep in?"

"Certainly I would, if I had permission."

Knowing that the room was practically in my grasp, I pointed to the phone. "Call your boss and see if you can get permission. If you can't get your boss, then it's obviously going to be up to you to decide what we should do."

Of course, she couldn't, or more than likely wouldn't, attempt to reach her boss at 1:30 in the morning. As a result, Ol' Barney moved into the Presidential Suite.

Overall, the entire evening ended up being a very interesting situation. You see, the corporate president of the company sponsoring the event wasn't in the Presidential Suite — Barney Zick lounged in it. The corporate president had a room down the hall in a Junior Suite. There was certainly no way the conference coordinator could fit this luxury room's exorbitant price into the conference budget. When the conference coordinator found out which room I was in, he made me swear to reveal my secret room to no one, especially not to the president. To cap off the story, I spent my entire conference stay in the Presidential Suite, but that's another story, isn't it?

Don't Forget to Negotiate

I have seen people repeatedly turned down for something that they deemed they should have received simply because they forgot or refused to negotiate. Forgetting to negotiate and refusing to negotiate are frequent excuses. Often, however, there are other reasons we fail, or at least fall short, in the negotiating art. Sometimes anger enters the picture. That's when it really gets interesting and, most of the time, gets you nothing in return. This generally occurs when you've been wronged, or at least think you have been wronged. You want the world to make it right. This is a primal instinct. It is NOT me. It's THEM. Do you recognize this person? What generally happens when you get mad, pound on the desk, act like a child, demand your way?

Such antagonistic responses leave little room, if any, for negotiation and often set up adversarial situations. Why go down that road? Good negotiators control emotions. There is nothing wrong with letting others know that you feel strongly about a situation, but never, ever, lose control. When it comes to negotiating business transactions, anger always gets in the way of communication. If you let emotions enter what would be an otherwise rational line of debate, you're making it difficult for others to communicate with you.

Had I blown my stack at the hotel clerk, I can absolutely assure you she would never have let me in the Presidential Suite or any suite, if she could help it. Without a room, I would have stayed for the meeting but would have, of necessity, been several blocks away. Just think of all that hiking back and forth to conference events. Instead, I spent the entire time in a gorgeous four-room suite with an outside sleeping area for my bodyguards (if I had bodyguards). Negotiation, my good friend, does pay.

I could continue with examples of what happens

when you *fail* to negotiate. You lose and lose and lose. I can see it now. You're remembering such events. Was it the time you had to report a sad story to your family, friends, or employer? Could the problem have been averted if you had remembered to use a few tactful negotiating skills? A Friendly Persuader would have controlled the situation and would have been keenly aware of what was acceptable and what should be avoided. Surely you're not one of those Pandy-Andy types who reserves asking for what you want after anger consumes you. Negotiate first, my friend. Don't get angry. Always remember that once you permit anger to surface, it is already too late to make any reasonable deal. You do remember the time you blew it, don't you? Well, from now on, you won't make that mistake again.

In every instance I've presented here, everyone was happy or content, except the man on his honeymoon, but that wasn't my fault, and the Marriott Hotel, but they deserved to lose my business because of their attitude. In fact, my Negotiating Nemesis generally feels better after we spend time negotiating. Negotiating isn't just taking something from the other person. A truly successful negotiation centers around finding out what the wants and needs of your Negotiating Nemesis are and then fulfilling those wants and needs in the best way you can while still keeping what is valuable to you. Even if your Nemesis is oblivious to your strategy, you paradoxically get *your personal needs met.* And, if it is a *truly successful* negotiated transaction, your Nemesis will have had wants and needs met, too. Before reading this book, you might have deemed negotiation either beneath you, unfair, or unkind.

Now, you know better, don't you?

Stay Calm

To negotiate effectively, learn to spend less time getting emotional and more time talking and listening. Make a *trade-off* within your own negotiating game plan. Trade anger for communication. The results will be less money left on the table and more money in your pocket.

Negotiation, then, is about giving:

➢ *More of yourself*

➢ *More of your talent*

➢ *More of your charm*

➢ *More of your energy*

➢ *More of your time*

Negotiating Is a Positive

Negotiating is not a negative. It is a positive. It stops arguments, stops fights, and stops misunderstandings. If, like the average Joe, you have some of these problems, negotiation simply helps you get along better in life. Momentarily allow me to again refer to the story of the London speaking engagement. Here, the convention manager and I both walked away feeling better. Since I had met and talked with this lady before, I knew she would rather not argue or haggle over price. I knew, too, that she preferred dealing with people who were easy to get along with. She essentially had two basic goals: (1) spend little time talking about price, and (2) confirm me to speak at a price within her budget. I actually received what I wanted, a trip to London at a conference that was beneficial to me, and I received it by giving her what she wanted, a well-known speaker who willingly, even anxiously, stayed within her budget. In a quiet and unthreatening negotiation, we both increased our level of satisfaction. This illustration is a perfect example of *The Negotiating Paradox* at work.

Before moving on, let's briefly summarize what we have learned.

> ➤ *Realize that you negotiate every day.*

> ➤ *Take time to learn the rules.*

> ➤ *Negotiate when you feel it is necessary or will help your cause or position.*

> ➤ *Negotiate everyday situations in ways beneficial to your position.*

> ➤ *Plan your strategy based on your goals, needs, and desires.*

> ➤ *And, of course, protect yourself to make sure no one takes advantage of you.*

By keeping these basic rules in mind, you can engage in skillful negotiations that increase the level of satisfaction for everyone, including yourself, while providing you and your Nemesis with a little more of what each person originally wanted. How easy does life get?

2
Hunting for the Best Solution

Is there a *best solution*? How do you define it? How do you know when you find it? The definition of the best solution is variable, and it simply depends upon what else is going on around you at that particular time. For some, the best solution may be to simply make a purchase at a reasonable price and go on with life. Remember the bass drum pedal? I wanted to purchase it quickly, cheaply, and within a specified time — right before Christmas.

At other times, the best solution requires more time, and some people value the time spent on seeking out better deals. The best solution for you, therefore, is what is contained in what YOU consider to be of most value, not what your Negotiating Nemesis values most. One person's junk is another's prize. A retired person values work. A working person values time. It's all relative to your wants, needs, desires, and goals.

You Pick and Choose

So, how do you negotiate for the best solution? As

I've pointed out, not every deal requires diligent negotiation. Once you master negotiation techniques and skills, you choose when and where to utilize them or make your own determination as to whether or not they are needed at that particular time. At times, you desire what is fast, easy, and quick. In the latter, time may be more important than money. A discount may be less important than getting what you want and going on with your day. In other instances, you use every ounce of your negotiation skills in order to improve your position. But, only you can determine what the best solution is for you at any given moment.

A very old, yet often unrecognized form of negotiation involves a universally misunderstood phenomenon—shopping. Nonshoppers and shoppers view the shopping icon differently, and the approach of both toward shopping clearly reveals these contrasts. Those shopping lovers travel from store to store. Dedicated to their mission, they spend time and enormous amounts of energy searching for the *Best Deal*. The *Best Deal* far outweighs the lowest price. It includes value, service, reliability, and other options. Those who detest shopping believe that *shop* is a four-letter word.

According to John Gray, author of the best-selling *Men Are from Mars, Women Are from Venus,* men are problem solvers, constantly hunting for the shortest path to the Best Solution. This concept might well explain why there may be more nonshoppers on the male side of the populace than on the female side.

In contrast to traditionl gender stereotyping, some women have developed a severe dislike for shopping, either out of necessity (time spent) or change of mind-set. However, some unchanged women absolutely love to shop, and shopping for them is more than a pastime. It is a vocation. It is what they do to stretch the family budget. It is what they do for themselves for personal satisfaction.

Although shopping lovers and haters are diverse and far ranging, they have one common goal when delving into a store. They have a problem to solve. Some find solutions, as Gray points out, quickly and conveniently. Others solve them over time and with a great deal of thought. Whatever method, both hunt for the best solution, and the best solution is what is best for them.

Let me use myself as a case in point. As a typical male shopper, I shop to solve a problem in a timely manner and then proceed with my busy day. Let's say that I discover my dress shoes are in bad shape. A brief examination shows them to be well worn and slightly scuffed. They have served me well (probably not long enough, but I am hard on shoes and like to keep up appearances). They have been as comfortable as, well, an old shoe. However, they are not candidates for further repair. Solution: I must have a new pair of shoes.

Within a day or week or month, depending upon when I get a chance, I stop at the nearest, most convenient, street level park-at-the-front-door establishment displaying a sign that in some manner convinces me it will have a new pair of shoes for me in the one and only brand I buy. When I enter the store, my voice and attention focus on what I assume to be a reasonably intelligent, willing, and mobile Negotiating Nemesis/sales clerk/order taker. I march straight ahead. "Just like these," I proudly intone without breaking my stride. "Black, size thirteen."

By the time I reach a chair, the Nemesis has disappeared into the back of the store. He returns in mere seconds with a box in hand and a slight smile on his face. "Exactly the same," are his first words. "Would you care to try them on?" Now, he's gearing up to negotiate, but he had not noticed that I had already removed my right shoe.

"Just the right one," I reply, reaching for the new shoe. Moments later I have it tied and stand to fully explore the feel. Then, I hit him with my brilliant negotiating counter punch.

"How much?"

"One-O-five, ninety-five," he answers. Was that a hind of perspiration on his forehead?

"I'll take them. MasterCard," I reply. "Just put them in a sack."

He rings up the transaction while I replace my old shoe. I sign the ticket and leave the store. We both say, "Thank you."

I'm sure most of you can relate to this scenario, recognizing yourself in one of these roles. You might ask, "How is it important?"   It certainly is not a good representation of negotiation, but it does illustrate that even in the most remote and unlikely situations, negotiation results from our efforts to find the best solution to everyday problems.

I had no time to negotiate price when my desire was simply to satisfy my immediate needs. I liked my old shoes. I was not interested in any other style, and I expected to pay in the specified price range. Since I hate to shop, I focused on leaving the store and getting back to work. I had no interest in going from store to store to save $2 or $8 or $18. My mind was concentrating on the next business deal.

If the clerk had tried to push another style off on me, even as wonderful as I am, I probably would have left the store — no sale made. My Nemesis was smart. He knew how to make that sale. He had seen people like me before. He merely had to satisfy the customer — me. Was I satisfied? Thoroughly. I walked out happily toting my shoes, the exact ones I wanted. Price was important, but not for shoes. I had business to conduct. Let's analyze the situation.

> *I wanted value.*

> *I got value.*

> *I wanted comfort.*

> *I got comfort.*

> *I wanted to get on my way.*

> *I was quickly on my way.*

> *I found the Best Solution for my problem.*

> *My problem was solved.*

> *Was I a happy camper?*

> *Sure was.*

World-Class Shoppers Go for the Tough Sale

True shoppers would consider my shopping

techniques clumsy and ineffectual. They approach shopping with more zest, gusto, umpf.

To dedicated shoppers, hunting for the best deal is, in part, to solve a problem or need. There, too, are those who shop just to be shopping. Depressed? Shop. Lonely? Shop. Tired? Happy? Feel like celebrating? Can't sleep? Broke? Shop...shop...shop.... Whatever their reasons, they go shopping, and whether or not they realize what they are doing, these so-called shopaholics are plunging themselves into the whirling midst of the world of negotiation every time they venture out in their avocation.

This is not to say that there is something amiss with these folks, nor are we assuming they are all women either. We all know dozens of men who go from store to store to find the best deal on fishing and hunting gear. The fact is these shoppers, male and female, often have something the rest of us lack — motivation to find the best solutions to their problems. For many of this group, the driving force is more of a compulsion than it is motivation. From my observation, shopaholics are, at times, the most business-oriented of all shoppers. For many of them, shopping has become a business within itself, and the rewards can be great. Smart shoppers save — 10%-20%-30%-50%-70%. Now, that's a good deal.

Regardless of why people shop and whether or not they realize the full implications of what they do, these otherwise savvy, business-oriented, fun-loving, shop-for-any-occasion, gotta-shop-till-they-drop individuals continue to plunge themselves, time after time, into the whirling midst of the negotiation world. If aware of effective negotiation techniques, these shoppers will more often than not succeed.

Shopperspouse

I have a good friend and business associate whom I will call Jim (in order to protect the innocent and preserve Jim's marriage). Jim affectionately refers to his wife of many years as Shopperspouse. According to Jim, Shopperspouse is a world-class shopper. She has the love, knack, and skill for shopping and is blessed (or cursed) with the one element many amateur shoppers lack — drive.

Shopperspouse is not extravagant. Jim says she never spends over her budget, and she never buys anything she doesn't want or need for herself or her family. She shops for the best solution, that is, the one that best satisfies her needs. She has to be absolutely certain she's made the best possible purchase, on the best possible terms and conditions, and at the best price.

Unlike amateur shoppers, this woman knows she is negotiating. To her, it is an art. She recognizes the various steps and stages involved in the negotiation process and, on her own, has mastered the steps and uses them to get what she wants.

Like any smart businessperson, Shopperspouse knows the market intimately and is fully aware of every style and brand that every store carries. Highly familiar with the pros and cons of the quality and reliability of each item, she recognizes the pricing structure of most department stores within a twenty-mile radius. She can handily outwit store managers at the drop of a hat and frequently does.

She calls her acquisitions *offs*. Jim has learned from experience never to insult his wife by asking the original price. The important issue from her point of view is the discount — the amount *off*. Instead of saying, "Let me

show you my purchases," she says, "Look at these *offs*."
Yes, *offs*, as in, "This is not a shopping bag; it's an *off*."
"This is not a sweater; it's an *off*."

Everything to this business-minded, bargain-driven Shopperspouse is relative to 40%, 60% or 70% off.

You see, this smart shopper never has and never will pay full price. Shopping is more than a game with her. It is a commitment.

Jim jokingly says the only mystery to him, after many years of observation, is that store management lets her in the door. "If I were the mall manager," Jim only half-jokingly says, "I would post a guard with a panoramic view of the parking lot near the entrance and instruct the guard to lock the front door if she approached. I've been with her (in one of my weak moments). I'll never again face the embarrassment. You see, when she strolls into a department store, looking from side to side, cruising the aisles with the keen eye of a customs inspector and the speed of a gazelle, I cringe. Those store clerks surely know by now that nothing misses her skillful eye. She targets every so-called sale and doesn't hesitate to point out the store's weak attempt at lowering prices. 'Just isn't worth the asking price,' is one of her favorite lines."

"In spite of those comments, virtually all store personnel smile, wave, and call greetings to her," Jim says. "All the while, my wife smiles back at them like Queen Elizabeth. And, she never slows her speed or neglects her mission. She moves ahead, all the while examining the merchandise and price tags along her appointed route."

"Carol," Shopperspouse calls out, "I see you still have this linen blouse in my size. Call me when it's 50% off."

Jim says he is astounded that store personnel continue to roll out the proverbial red carpet for her in spite of one of her favorite shopping techniques—returning items. Shopperspouse believes making up her mind is simply a part of the standard operating procedure in the shopping process. Her definition of making up her mind involves having an initial interest in the product, making an initial selection as to color and size, acquiring the item, and taking it home. Over the next few hours or days, she contemplates her decision. Only when she gets it home does she really determine whether she wants or needs the item and whether or not she intends to *really* purchase it. If so, she proudly announces to Jim that the transaction is permanent. Otherwise, she simply returns it.

Jim firmly believes that his wife has more experience refolding and repackaging store merchandise than all the clerks in the mall combined. And, her return policy is forthright and uncomplicated. She will return merchandise if she wants to return merchandise. Simple. Remember, I said *her* return policy. She feels the store's return policy is merely a guideline for those less proficient at the game. It doesn't concern her at all.

Jim reports that while paying the household bills one Saturday a few years back, he asked Shopperspouse how it was possible that she had a credit balance of $354 at Department Store A.

"Simple," she said with confident logic. "When I was purchasing new household linens, I gathered two colors of my brand from Store A, Store B, and my favorite Store C to get the quantity and selection we needed."

True to form, she brought them all home and then chose one color over the other. All linen selections of the rejected color, therefore, had to be returned. Rather than go back to all three stores, she simply returned all items of the rejected color to Store A because, as she explained without blinking, "Store A's price was higher on the same thing, so I got a larger credit." Now, how can anyone argue with logic like that?

"But, how can you do that," Jim asked, "without proper sales slips from Store A?"

"Oh, they know me," she replied. "Besides, they know I'll be back."

With that remark, she illustrates why her shopping/ negotiating technique works. It could work for everyone.

Shopperspouse is an effective negotiator:

➢ *She hunts for the Best Solution.*

➢ *She knows what she wants.*

➢ *She knows what she is willing to pay.*

➢ *She knows what is important to her.*

➢ *Her family gets the finest product at the lowest possible price.*

➢ *Stores get return business.*

➢ *She is likeable and easy to sell to when the price is right.*

➢ *She is a buyer.*

The clerk knows she will buy the blouse when, and

if, the price is reduced 50%. At such a time, the clerk makes the call. The sale is made. The store moves the merchandise. The clerk makes commission.

Store managers realize that anything Shopperspouse returns is store-ready. Her repackaging would fool even the factory. The store recognizes that this woman's *Hunting for the Best Solution* concurrently results in what is the best solution for them as well. She is a good customer, steady buyer, and competent shopper who knows what she wants and willingly pays a fair price for it.

Choose Success

Successful negotiators, such as Jim's wife, are successful because they choose success. In addition, they prepare properly and expect to be winners. Preparation for anything worthwhile takes time and planning. Life is a process. Short-circuiting the process short circuits success. Think about that wedding you prepared for your son or daughter or that new car you purchased last year. Did you leave those events up to chance?

Let's use the wedding as an example. What would happen if you just decided to show up at the church at 2 p.m. for your daughter's wedding? Without prior planning, the church doors could be locked. The minister might be snoozing. It *is* Sunday afternoon. Let's say your daughter is in law school. Wouldn't she be studying? No cake, no flowers, and no guests would be there. Not even the bride and groom would show up without advance preparations. If planning for a wedding requires time and commitment (and, of course, we all know it takes an inordinate amount of each), why wouldn't you put the same energy into negotiating for what you want in all other important matters of your day-to-day life?

At the wedding rehearsal, every team player knows where to stand, what to say, and when to say it. A negotiating team (and you may be the negotiating team) needs the same ground rules. Know in advance what your every action and move will be.

Always be prepared, though, for the unexpected. If the unexpected does occur, know your counter moves. Know what your Negotiating Nemesis wants, and be prepared to offer it. This preparation allows you to win.

Where Do We Learn Negotiating Skills?

The sad reality is that few are aware of the negotiation process and fewer still have had formal training or coaching that will help them learn negotiating skills. I often wonder how we are expected to pick up such skills. On our own? On the job? What an expensive, time-consuming, and frustrating way to learn. I call this process *Learn by Losing*.

My business friend and a former practicing attorney, Doug Gilliss, agrees with me. After practicing law for several years, Doug noticed a pronounced shortcoming in his training. Doug routinely dealt with other attorneys and clients to solve legal, economic, or business problems. His training had taught him that problems were best solved through formal legal procedures called litigation, and in case you haven't figured it out by now, that's spelled e-x-p-e-n-s-i-v-e.

Doug readily noticed the enormous expense and counter-productive effects of such procedures, so he began to keep track of the cases that could be, or should have been, resolved through mediation, a legal term for negotiation, instead of through a lawsuit or costly trial.

Doug soon discovered that more than three out of four disputes, a whopping 75%, could be partially or fully resolved through negotiation or at least some type of reasonable communication. Stark reality sat in when Doug discovered that instead of legal counsel, his clients, in many instances, simply craved an objective person to listen or help them communicate better or more effectively. In all cases, they could have better managed their situations if either party had been aware of the art of negotiation.

Unresolved business problems and disputes simply need to be worked out. If one person in a dispute is adept in negotiation, most problems are resolved without a lawyer. Clearly, negotiation can easily replace litigation in many instances. The former is less expensive and more productive.

Which Table?

Doug discovered this solution worked equally well in everyday matters that are far less important. In a restaurant, do you sit at the table by the window or by the restroom door? Whether confronted with a business dispute or table selection, a simple solution without litigation and without time-consuming frustration is readily at hand.

Management Carries Authority

Hunting for the best solution involves the application of management, and management implies that one has the *ability and the authority* to manage.

Therefore, when you negotiate, you manage a situation. You are pro-active. You are in charge. You are the manager. As such, you plan, organize, and control the situation.

People Versus Computers

Wouldn't it be nice to negotiate with a computer? Computers do not think; they are exact. They respond only to input and data programmed into them. To negotiate with a computer successfully, we could plug in desired responses and simply ask the computer questions for ready-made answers. Of course, we would pre-program so that all solutions would be favorable to us. Would this process be challenging or satisfying? Probably not.

Unlike negotiating with a computer, successful negotiation leaves both sides feeling satisfied, content, and ready for the next deal. There is little doubt that we are truly at a disadvantage when negotiating with people. Unlike computers, PEOPLE can disagree with us. They get emotionally involved in responses. They misconstrue our intentions. They nag. They bicker. They have a bad hair day, need warm fuzzies, get sick, tired, and they may even occasionally be overworked.

To top it off, humans form a rationale all their own, and quite often that rationale makes little sense to us. It doesn't matter. After all, it's *their* rationale, and we must negotiate around it. Since humans are complex and have many complex emotions, it is no small wonder that we find it challenging to negotiate with them.

Challenging? Yes. Tough? Frequently. But, negotiate we must.

Be Forewarned and Prepared

Buying decisions are, in part, emotional. We must be aware of our own emotions as well as the emotions of others in any negotiation. Thus, like communication skills, language skills, and social skills, negotiation is a business and economic skill. Those poorly trained, for example, in language or speaking skills suffer professionally and personally. Many fail to even realize the magnitude of their loss, yet others recognize it and frequently will take advantage of any weakness or shortcoming if they are not stopped.

Develop Your Negotiation Skills

Since many of you realize you lose if poorly trained in reading, writing, and communication, you have taken appropriate steps to increase your chances of success by polishing those skills through formal education or professional training courses. Some may think it's unfair to be judged because they lack specific skills. Remember, no one ever told us that life is fair. Life is reality.

In most cultures and civilizations, there are winners and losers. We expect both, so it is no wonder that untrained negotiators often try too hard to win. We have all, at some time or other, heard some executives refer to their customers as the opposition.

Negotiation is not about winning and losing. It isn't a ball game that ends after four quarters. It is about establishing a mutually beneficial relationship that you want to last beyond the single deal. To cement relationships and preserve benefits for all concerned parties, the *win-lose* philosophy simply doesn't work.

As a more effective approach, we are exploring how to satisfy our needs by meeting our Nemesis' needs. The result is more satisfaction for both sides. A word of caution is in order. This unique method does require you to invest enough time and energy to discover your negotiating strategy. You start by listing all items or services you can possibly place on the negotiating table. Make sure these are items you can forfeit and are willing to give up. How can you remove offerings if they are absolutely necessary to your side? Be sure, though, to never place your credibility on the negotiation table. You must implement an ample amount of public relations work before and during the introductory phase of the negotiations. This self-promoting insures that no one ever doubts your ability and desire to execute every detail you include in the transaction.

3

Negotiating Is More Than Bargaining

How does negotiating compare to bargaining? Actually, most people bargain when they think they are negotiating. Bargaining means simply arguing over price. You go back and forth.

If buying a car, and the other party says, "It's $20,000."

You say, "I'll give you $18,500."

They say, "$19,000."

In this situation, you are arguing over a single aspect of the deal. This dickering reduces the negotiation to something less than favorable. How can either side win if for every dollar the Nemesis receives, the Friendly Persuader must forfeit that same dollar? That's not really negotiating. It is bargaining (or arguing) over price. Sometimes this technique is called *haggling*. As a technique, it at least dates back to street vendors who used it during the early days of the Roman Empire. It is a simple, straightforward, tried-and-true procedure that permits you to request more than you expect to get. The other party offers less than he or she is prepared to give. When haggling, make certain you clearly understand each other. Don't obfuscate. Always express yourself clearly in a language everyone understands.

Wheeling and Dealing

Have you ever been to the tourist markets of a Mexican border town and negotiated the purchase of a big, pointed sombrero or a colorful blanket? Even if you haven't had the pleasure, you have probably heard of a friend's experience. The exchange is familiar.

"How much?"

The Mexican peddler says, "Twenty dollars."

"Too much. No more than five." The American begins to walk away.

The Mexican yells out a lower price, with a tag line of, "Just for you, my friend." The American cheerfully smiles and buys the hat for $7.50.

"Really got him down," the American thinks.

Sound familiar? These bastions of pure free-enterprise wheeling and dealing bring out the spirited bargainer in all of us. I'll admit it. I have found myself bargaining for goods I didn't really want and couldn't use. (Have you ever seen anyone wearing a hat haggled from one of these "poor" Mexican street vendors?) Just think about it. That "poor" Mexican peddler has *never* sold one of those hats for the original asking price of $20. He never intended to. That "poor" peddler probably pays $4.50 per hat and sells 30 or 40 a day on the beach to those tough gringo negotiators. Now, who is really the Friendly Persuader?

While vacationing, it's all good sport, and the locals

expect your zealous haggling, but don't confuse haggling with the more important business and personal transactions we encounter daily. Usually, there's no take-it-or-leave-it bartering in our more serious transactions. It is almost always counterproductive.

When Do You Negotiate?

Now, if you're thinking Barney expects you to haggle over the price of a carton of milk at the supermarket, you can relax. I don't. Nor do I expect you to throw out your suppliers' price lists and start advancing lowball offers for the valuable services or materials they provide you. You might find yourself surrounded with offended *ex-suppliers*. Recreational, south-of-the-border bargaining isn't the answer for everyday purchases.

All too often many people equate any negotiation to bargaining or haggling. Such thinking is unfortunate. There's more to almost every deal than simply arguing over price. You can negotiate for more time with your spouse or kids, a more favorable work environment, better accommodations, and many other goods and services. You can even negotiate for a better quality of life.

Some make the mistake of claiming to be highly experienced negotiators when in actuality all they do is bargain, and this is usually over price. Are they better off than those who fail to negotiate? I would say, "No."

Americans Want Quick Fixes

Perhaps we in America are inept at real negotiations because we have grown to want and expect speedy results in everything we do. This can be a useful trait, at times, but it usually is somewhat unrewarding. Yes, it may be great fun haggling over the price of a chess set in Mexico. Haggling or bargaining price is a fast, easy way to get what you want. It takes a few minutes to either make the purchase or forget it. If you purchase the item, it is yours. Did you outsmart the poor Mexican peddler? No way. He knows what to charge and how to negotiate for the price he needs. So, what did you really gain? Nothing, unless you enjoyed the exercise.

Easy doesn't necessarily equate to winning, does it? When dealing with the Mexican peddler, easy is just a trick to get you to play the game. I recall a quotation: "There are always two choices — two paths to take. One is easy. And its only reward is that it is easy."

An effective negotiator goes beyond easy. A Friendly Persuader realizes that the more time and effort spent on a deal, the higher the payoff; and the bigger the deal, the more time and effort it will take. If you go to the negotiation table and merely haggle over price, you will more than likely lose more than you gain. Which side of the table is more appealing? The winning side? The losing side? The winning side, of course.

You Can Lose Your Negotiation Power

To win you must keep your negotiating power strong. Sometimes we have the tendency to talk too much, and talking too much weakens our negotiation stance. A classic example occurred when a couple sold a house and had only a fixed amount of time to reinvest the money before paying taxes on the profit. If they reinvested in another equally priced or more expensive house, they could defer the tax. If they waited too long, they would have to pay tax on the profit made from the first house no matter which house they bought. This couple foolishly put themselves into the position of having only one month to buy a house to avoid unnecessary taxes.

To their disadvantage, the couple announced their problem to every property owner they encountered (the couple's Negotiating Nemesis). Price was the couple's primary concern. They could afford to pay $10,000, $20,000, or even $30,000 extra on the house because they were looking at more than $30,000 in taxes. Since every Negotiating Nemesis knew price was the couple's main concern, do you think this couple was able to get a price break? Not on your life. They paid in excess because they had a short time to complete the deal. This couple lost negotiating power simply because they focused on price and offered too much information. Focusing only on price has and always will be a mistake.

Keep Your Eyes off Price

Too much attention focused on price is usually detrimental to effective negotiations. I remember a situation in Kansas City where a major insurance company attempted to buy property to expand a parking lot. When the manager spoke with the seller, he discussed only price.

The owner of the property, Wayne, said he wanted $100,000 for the property. The insurance company offered $95,000, a figure which was based on a recent property appraisal. From the insurance company's point of view, the price was $95,000 or nothing.

When You Bother to Ask

Did the insurance company purchase the desired property? No. They walked away from the deal. A friend of mine, (let's call him Frank) later bought the property for $100,000. Frank, a skilled Friendly Persuader, took the time to ask his Negotiating Nemesis a simple but important question: "Why are you stuck on this price?"

The Negotiating Nemesis said, "Well, I've got it all figured out. If I sell it, I can finance it myself. I don't need a down payment. I don't need any payment for the first three years. I'm retiring six years from now, and if I earn 6% on $100,000 — that's just the right amount."

With that knowledge, my friend knew the needs of his Negotiating Nemesis and met those needs. Had Frank focused only on price, his negotiation efforts would have failed. The insurance company did fail by walking away at the $100,000 asking price. The company could probably have paid more than $100,000 and still come out ahead. My friend bought the property with no payment for three years at 6% financing, fully amortized over twenty-seven years. He paid the $100,000 and received a right of substitution of collateral. He took that substitution of collateral, moved it to another piece of property he owned, and sold the property for $95,000 to the insurance company. To Frank, this deal was equal to borrowing $95,000 on a long-term note at six percent per annum.

Frank, in short, bought the availability of a loan. He bought the financing at what equated to little more than 7% actual interest for three years. As Frank related, "You can't usually borrow $95,000 with payment terms as good as those."

Frank was an effective Friendly Persuader. He asked the right questions and found out what the Negotiating Nemesis most valued. He easily met that need. That, my friend, is a beautiful example of *The Negotiating Paradox* at work.

Be a Smart Negotiator

A Friendly Persuader is a smart negotiator. You are now in that role. When you negotiate, you move from arguing over one aspect of a deal to finding out what is important to your Negotiating Nemesis. This path moves you toward successful transaction closings and leaves both parties satisfied.

By now you should have a more rational attitude toward negotiations. The rest of the book targets practical advice that will move you toward personal and financial success.

4

A Simple System for Negotiating Success

Today it seems that almost everyone in the corporate world is under budgetary pressure. Too often company representatives who are placed in charge of hundreds of thousands of corporate acquisitions have little, if any, negotiating skills. Erroneously, old school negotiators often believe that price outweighs all else. Smart buyers recognize that a company's long-term goals and the vendors' true needs and motivations are most important. Shortsighted buyers not only miss out on front-end bargains, but they also miss the benefit of a productive long-term relationship with quality vendors. No Friendly Persuader will ever be accused of being shortsighted.

Five Step Program to Success

If you are to be truly successful in your new achievement of Friendly Persuader status, there are two basic strategies that are paramount. You must first change your overall attitude about your approach to negotiating as a way of life. Secondly, you must master the new techniques and strategies that we have outlined. Without understanding negotiating strategies, you will seldom realize when someone, or a company, manipulates you. That lack of knowledge could cost you or your firm millions of dollars. Despite numerous seminars, books, and tapes on negotiating strategies, most individuals either lack a system or they tend to over-complicate the system.

Confusion exists partially because many negotiating techniques rely far too heavily on numerous steps and strategies that overwhelm the average person. It's like trying to unwind plastic wrap. You don't know where or how to begin.

The *Negotiating Paradox* breaks the process into five basic focus areas. This simple and clear plan enables you to successfully tap into a reservoir of creative problem-solving techniques that will ensure success. To expand your knowledge in any area, you need only to examine those techniques more fully. Mastering negotiation techniques boosts profits and increases consumer satisfaction while making you a stronger seller or buyer.

STEP ONE: Be Clear about Desired Outcome

If you prefer fancy jargon, you might call this internal needs and goals analysis. One approach to analyzing your needs is the *Mini-Max* approach. This technique, used in many disciplines, such as science, statistics, and business, helps you to better understand your primary goals.

In order to open yourself to insights and possibilities, you might try this mental exercise. Imagine that Santa is standing in front of you with his wish list. He owes you one, and he's in a jolly mood. What would you ask for? What are the hidden benefits and extra goodies that would come from the best win you could ever possibly imagine?

Visualize the best possible outcome. Too often people concentrate on what they hope will happen. Hope is generally halfway between your wildest expectations and your worst fears. Concentrate on the best thing that can happen. Think of all the endless possibilities. Spend time mentally seeing these opportunities in full detail.

Psychologists tell us that visualization has value. Strong mental images take on reality. You are, in effect, what you think. If you skip the visualization of your wildest expectations, you automatically reduce greatly your odds of obtaining what you desire from life.

Greg Norman is a perfect example. When he was asked how he blew the PGA title in 1996 after years and years of being acknowledged as the top golfer in the world, he reluctantly admitted that when he started finding fault with his game, he lost confidence. His mental game set his upward limits just as you set yours.

Have you ever wondered why some people always seem to succeed? Perhaps they planned on success and then set out to find success. Though unaware, you may often face defeat simply because you planned to achieve defeat. That "I can't win attitude" costs you. Take it from me. If you say you can't win, you assuredly *will not*.

Besides being psychologically beneficial, visualization is technically important. How can you know what to ask for without knowing the possibilities? How can you know the small items to request without a clear understanding of your desire? When you better understand your true primary wants and needs, your negotiation arena widens to include a larger playing field. A wider playing field increases the odds of success.

Next, look at the worst possible outcome. Don't dwell on this part or expect the worst to happen. Just take a factual look at the worst possible outcome and move on.

Analyzing the worst possible outcome may help you realize that your worst fears *ain't all that bad*. Needless fear blows things out of proportion. The more you worry, the more you find to worry about. Before long, nothing seems to work or fall in place.

Examining the negative permits alternative solutions to surface and allows you to easily abandon your worst fears. It is far easier to distance yourself from a negative situation when you realize that a "Plan B" or alternative solution exists.

Recognizing other positions will strengthen your creative energy and your negotiating stance. Of course, it is vitally important to be aware of problems and issues. Just don't allow fear to override your ability to see choices.

Be Empowered

A positive attitude actually heightens your awareness of solutions. You'll feel a unique sense of personal empowerment. You'll suddenly see creative alternatives that others miss.

Certainly, most powerful negotiators have consciously or subconsciously broken the chains of negativity. They know the importance of positive thinking, and they know their alternatives. When you recognize that you have choices, you will no longer view success as an accidental by-product and will better understand how success comes to those who deliberately exercise learned skills.

Sometimes company representatives find themselves going into a negotiation saying, "No matter what, we need to get *X* or we can't make a deal." Or, "Wow, if we could get Y, our year would be made." Admit it. You've been there.

Realistically this thinking is flawed. When you thoroughly analyze the highs and lows of any situation, you will see that you can almost always assess the issues more clearly and better visualize your more *likely* desirable outcome.   In this case, I'm not just stressing desirable outcome — but the *most likely desirable outcome.* The goal you *most desire* is the one you want to achieve.

Since we tend to get what we expect out of life, I encourage you to expect a very wonderful outcome and work toward achieving it.   The old saying, "Expect the worst, and you'll seldom be disappointed," is oh, so true.

Knowing exactly what it is that you desire is equally important. When you know what you want, then go for it at full speed.

As you work through this first but valuable step (before the big face-to-face meeting), it is important to get a handle on the highest, lowest, most likely, and most desirable outcomes. The most likely goal will now become your worst goal, the one you will settle for only if no better opportunity arises to improve your position. For now, that may be the case, but as you master specific negotiation skills, you'll learn ways to easily advance your negotiation stance. Remember that you've only taken step one.

Examine, Examine, Examine

When analyzing personal goals, be sure to include the goals of your boss or partner, banker, spouse, or any other party with a stake in the outcome. Weigh these opinions or positions to see if any of them are important to you or to the deal.

If you are an employee, the primary outcome could be performing better than the boss expects. It could be that this is so integral to your day-to-day tasks that only you will know the difference if you do a better job or worse job. Regardless, factor all of this information into your analysis. Examine it from various angles. Explore every possibility.

If, on the other hand, you are part of a firm, you should know what is important to the company. Don't let personal ambition or enthusiasm override logical decisions. Listen to others and evaluate their input and concerns. Then, make a final analysis based on personal *and* company needs.

When analyzing needs, always keep supply and demand factors in focus. If negotiating for a new bedroom addition for Mom when she gets out of the hospital, then time factors are crucial. If needing the bedroom for a child you hope to have next year, then you're not "under the gun" as my granddad, a Texas cowboy at the turn of the century, would have said. If you can't meet a deadline, change it rather than miss it and lose your credibility.

Finally, ask yourself these questions: "What do I want from this deal? What am I willing to put into it? What special services or talents can I place on the negotiation table?" (Include here such items as reliability, reputation, warranty, and service.) "What are my parameters? What can I do or not do? How high or how low can I or will I go in order to get what I want from my Negotiating Nemesis in this particular negotiation or transaction?" At this point, we are taking a broader perspective, a first look, so ask yourself a multitude of questions and come up with a variety of answers. Once you have answers, weigh them *so very carefully* before you make your decision.

You should endlessly detail your list since each situation will have a unique set of characteristics. For now, just remember that the critical first step is to know yourself, know the details of the negotiation at hand, and know the possibilities of the various outcomes.

Let's pause for a moment and summarize the important questions to ask yourself during this critical first step.

> *What do I want from this deal?*

> *What am I willing to give up?*

> *What can I bring to the negotiation table, other than the obvious — money or product? (Here be sure to list such items as reliability, reputation, warranty, and service.)*

> *What are my parameters?*

> *What can I do or not do?*

> *How high will I go to get what I want?*

> *How low will I go? It is important to keep all negotiations in perspective.*

These are serious and thought provoking questions that will enable you to get a broader perspective of your unique situation, and by actually itemizing them, you can expand that view even more. Use them, and they will help you develop your negotiation plan.

STEP TWO: Know Your Opponents Better than They Know Themselves. (Remember That It Takes Two to Tango.)

In any negotiation and at any level of intensity, if there is an issue worthy of your involvement, there are counterpoints held by others who believe in their cause, are willing to defend their position against you, and are ready to take what you own to enhance their strength, holdings, pride or satisfaction. In battle, it's the enemy. In sports, it's the opponent. In marriage, it's the spouse. (No! No! Just kidding.) In negotiation, it's the Negotiating Nemesis. To negotiate effectively, you need to know your opponents better than they know themselves.

Don't Be Detoured by Corporate Hype

If you really know your Nemesis, you will never undermine that person's integrity or status or that of his or her company. It is not uncommon for those in the middle of a situation to fail to see the full spectrum of their position. Some companies artfully disfigure their employee's perspective of job opportunities or permanency of company positions. An example would be major employers who often hype company and product merits to the point of making a few marketing and salespeople believe no competition exists.

Years ago, in one of our country's first large corporate downsizings, when some were terminated from IBM, they were shocked at their dismissal. Their training and expertise allowed them to easily obtain other jobs, but IBM had so convinced them that IBM was *it* in computers that these blinded folks literally could not imagine working for anyone else.

Corporate hype can detour your thinking. Yet, longer vacations, impressive titles, larger facilities, and bigger staffs do little for you when the company shuts the door. To find out what really goes on in business or life, go to the Internet, the library, or the barber or beauty shop and talk with and about competitive suppliers. If necessary, talk to your neighbors. Talk, talk, talk, in order to learn, learn, learn.

Read the Footnotes First

I will be honest. I have always been reluctant to march up to a neighbor's door and ask for negative information on the people next door. I always had someone else do it. Luckily for me, my former spouse was great at such things. No fear. No reluctance. If she needed information about a house in a neighborhood and she knew nothing of the neighborhood, the neighbor, or the house, she would march up to any door and ring the bell.

Since I was too embarrassed to knock on a stranger's door and ask unsolicited questions, I observed the conversation from a distance. But, after a while, my curiosity would get the best of me, and I would get out of my car and join them. What in heaven's name could they be talking about anyway?

From listening, I soon discovered that my wife started such conversations by talking about the neighborhood. Next, she subtly moved to asking, "Is this a good place to live?" The conversation then turned to the neighbors. Eventually the dialogue settled on the specific neighbor and the house that was for sale. "Oh, my!" and "You're kidding!" were common utterances.

You can use this same approach when you need information about competitors. Questioning competitors in a business situation may not always get you immediate, usable feedback, but when you have reached the point where competitors trust you, boy, do they open up. In a short time, you will learn more about the competition than you expected — their financial situation, their personnel problems, their successes, and their failures. All you have to do is ask questions and attentively listen.

The same rule applies when examining financial statements of public companies. I learned a trick from one of my college professors — *read the footnotes first!* If you initially read that a company is fighting thirty-two discrimination suits, the president's statement in the front of the annual report that reads "The firm has instituted a study panel on cultural diversity in the workplace" takes on new meaning.

If, for example, you were in the business of diversity training, and you had only read the first few pages of the report, you would know nothing of the true character of that company. Lack of valuable information can prevent you from negotiating what is best for you. Don't needlessly give the other party the upper hand. It is your job to know all you can know before entering into negotiations of any kind. With proper knowledge, you can decide if and when you want to negotiate. The cards are in your hand, as they should be.

It Is Your Job to Interview

Another positive way to gain information is to interview. Interviewing provides information quickly and economically, and if properly planned, this technique may unfold a wealth of valuable information.

To be effective, the interviewing process is ideally broken into two steps.

> ➢ *If time permits, interview once to gather facts and admit nothing.*

> ➢ *After you have had a chance to fit what you learned into what you already know, go back into the negotiation and seriously negotiate.*

This two-fold interview process may not always be possible, but often you can arrange a meal with your Nemesis the evening before your official meeting, or you might schedule the meeting an hour before lunch and plan to continue the negotiation dialogue afterwards.

Although these options are not always possible and certainly not always necessary, I advise using them until you are fully equipped with negotiation skills or until you can think quickly through a situation. Having additional time to assess your client's or customer's wants and needs can be helpful because informal mealtime meetings enable you and your Negotiating Nemesis to relax. Once relaxed, your Negotiating Nemesis will reveal traits, thoughts, mannerisms, personality quirks, desires, and goals you will never get from a formal business meeting. In this setting, you readily find out if your opponent is seriously interested in making this deal, and if so, what exactly is necessary from you to complete it, other than money or goods.

Let's say your client is head x-ray technician in a large hospital, and you are negotiating for the hospital to consider purchasing your company's five million dollar CAT scan equipment. What would persuade the technician to encourage the hospital to purchase from you rather than your competition?

Over a leisurely dinner or a game of golf, you could more than likely find out what the competition is offering and what goods, services, or warranties were included in those deals. With this information, you could surely find one extra service that could benefit the hospital or the technician. Does your new fancy machine process higher quality images in less time? Exactly what sets your machine apart from similar machines?

Take time to find out precisely what the technician needs from this equipment that hasn't been offered. Then, focus on that factor or benefit during your negotiation. You want to make the sale. The technician wants the best quality machine and the best service for the money.

From this point , your job is easy. You are now prepared to show the technician that your machine is the best quality machine for the money and that your service is the best. By allowing your client to inadvertently help you design your sales pitch, you move toward a smoother close. A smoother close assures you that you and your Nemesis will both be more content.

STEP THREE: What Makes You Unique?

With all the beef out there, you must strive to be the sauce. Competition is fierce. The stakes are high. You can't just be part of the pack. You have to be the leader of the pack, the head honcho, the top layer of cheese. You might be the most creative or have the most convenient product or have the fastest turn around time or offer the lowest financing cost. Regardless of what you offer, always strive to be unique. Forget being just another sales manager. Be the best sales manager, the unique one who fulfills the needs of others.

Once you've established your unique traits, forget them. You heard me right. Push them momentarily aside, and focus on your Nemesis. Does your Nemesis see any unique traits in you? If you can highlight those qualities to your opponent, you have a better chance of closing a deal at the negotiation table. Remember that your Nemesis is only negotiating with you to solve a problem. If you can solve that problem, you have become unique in that person's eyes.

From this point forward in the negotiation process, your Nemesis' perception is the only perception that matters. Satisfying your customer's or client's needs must remain your top priority. If a client needs a faster turn around time, offer that service and stress that point during the negotiation. You waste valuable time discussing deferred payments if turn around time is your client's main concern. If on the other hand, you solve the problem, then you are truly unique in your Nemesis' eyes. Being unique gives you the leverage you need to negotiate effectively.

Oats Are Oats

Advertisers realize the importance of making their products unique. Advertisers carefully craft commercials that focus on consumers' needs, and by so doing, they elevate their products in the eyes of consumers.

Remember the popular oatmeal commercial a few years ago? In this ad Mom sends her little son (let's call him Johnny) out in the cold. He is bundled up, and the food he just consumed (oatmeal) will keep him warm throughout the day.

In reality, oatmeal is oatmeal, but the commercial encourages you to believe that this particular oatmeal is unique because it warms your kids. The advertisers never claim that their oatmeal tastes better than other brands or that it is of superior quality.

Doesn't all hot food warm you on the inside? Of course it does, but this campaign works because the warm connotation strikes a subconscious chord. When Mom sees this particular box of oatmeal in a store, she will subconsciously think of warm food, and she associates that warmth with nourishing food — the kind Grandma used to make. She is made to believe that *her oatmeal* is some good, old fashioned food. Instead it is something quick and easy that, though good for her little darling, does nothing to help keep him warm. It is the association with the warm image that makes this oatmeal unique over other brands in Mom's eyes.

These advertisers knew better than to waste time trying to convince Moms that one particular brand of oatmeal has a better taste than others. Oatmeal tastes like oatmeal. They just found a way, through their advertising campaign, to separate *the perception* of their oatmeal from other brands. In doing so, their oatmeal is unique.

To devise this campaign, the advertisers had to do one thing — mentally climb inside the heads of all those Moms. They realized that the desire of all busy mothers is to serve their families nourishing, easy-to-prepare food. These Moms care about their children. They want to serve nourishing food, and they want to keep their children warm on cold winter days.

The smile on every face tells the story. Little Johnny is happy. Mom is happy. The oatmeal manufacturer and its advertising agency are happy, too.

As a Friendly Persuader, this same approach will work for you. Before negotiating, know your Nemesis' wants and needs. Then, faithfully set out to fulfill them. It's that simple.

So, when establishing your plan, emulate advertisers who mentally climb inside the heads of their clients. Ask relevant questions and listen intently for answers. Remember that if your customer wants apples, give them the finest tasting apples. When that person needs apples again, that person will come to you.

Colonel Sanders

Kentucky Fried Chicken built an entire industry on providing people with what they wanted — fried chicken as a fast food. Before the fast food fried chicken era, this entrée was mainly reserved for Sunday meals. Colonel Sanders' company had smart negotiators.

The Colonel's chicken appeared on the American scene just as Moms started working more outside the home. Naturally, they had less time or desire to cook. This company recognized that fried chicken remained a favorite food despite Moms' busy schedules.

The company set out to give customers what was most desired — delicious fried chicken, anytime, any day, and at a reasonable price.

It worked.

It all turns back to assessing your competitor's needs. When you fulfill needs, you align yourself as a unique individual who focuses on solving problems.

Doctors and other professionals have aligned themselves this way. When sick, we seek the advice of medical doctors because we believe they are in a unique position. We believe or hope that they have the expertise and knowledge to make us well.

Although doctors can't always meet these expectations, people, on the whole, perceive them in this role. As a result, when we become ill, we go to our doctor. Generally speaking, we never think of this person at any other time. How many times have you just decided to drop by the doctor's office to read magazines or chat with patients in the waiting room? Perception is everything.

Get sick? Go to the doctor.

Align Your Position

Likewise, marketers who can identify their uniqueness and can apply consumer-aligned positioning usually corner markets. Too many client representatives depend on the low prices or the company's reputation to carry sales. Those who learn to position themselves in a manner that identifies their uniqueness and competitive advantage with their product or services will reap the rewards.

To lock in a sale, make your Nemeses think that you and only you can solve a problem for them. You have the finest apples. You have the best oatmeal. You have the most reliable computer. It works for advertisers, and it will work for you.

This strategy works because it automatically shifts strength to your side of the negotiation table. It places the ball in your court and allows you the advantage of making the next move. Being unique in your Nemesis' eyes does not mean you exude great charm or take on a false identify. Great charm and deception will do little to sell products, goods, or services.

While there is nothing wrong with being charming, don't rely entirely on charm when your client needs faster service or an extended warranty. A more effective approach is to concentrate on what your client needs.

If It Ain't Broke, Don't Fix It

First and foremost, find out what needs or services your clients desire. *If it ain't broke, don't fix it.* Fix what is broken to make a sale. It is your job to market products so that clients recognize the added benefits or solutions that directly affect their lives, their emotions, their needs, and their desires. Your product or service must ultimately benefit them. Only then do you move toward a signed deal. As holder of a product or service, aggressively market yourself as the person uniquely able to fulfill a need. Remember that you are now the coach. Take charge and coach the team. We have frequently been talking about *perception* as being an important factor. At this critical stage of the negotiation, perception is all that matters. Your personal identity is of little concern to your Negotiating Nemesis. Regardless of your charm and ability to flatter, don't be fooled into thinking that your emotional satisfaction will win clients to your side. Give up this utopian idea before it leads to frustration and failure. The only effective way to make sales is to satisfy customers' or clients' emotional or material needs. When focusing on your core functions—your ambition or your originality—you quickly lose sight of your client's needs. In such instances, your personal bottom line will suffer.

By all means, never lose sight of your identity for your own benefit. You're the same person who shaved or put on make-up several hours earlier. Keeping in touch with reality is vital to your success.

Keep in mind that you still have the same goal or objective that must be achieved as a result of the impending negotiation. That has not and should not change. Shifting focus to your Nemesis' point of view merely helps you understand the other side's motives and objectives. You then set your counter-motives and counter-objectives.

By knowing your Negotiating Nemesis, by mentally climbing into that person's head for a moment, you assess your own position from your client's perspective. You mentally prioritize your strengths and present those in the order and format that your Nemesis most values. What your client most values becomes your strength. This strength is what makes you uniquely valuable.

Keep in mind that your Nemesis' perception is more important than your actuality. To survive and thrive in the negotiation world, you need to market yourself and your company in some unique way that is worthwhile to clients and customers. Failing to negotiate, based on your uniqueness and your Nemesis' true needs and motivation, may cause you to lose a sale and a client. Lose enough sales and clients, and you are out of business. To avoid losing, spend time finding out what makes you and your products unique. The time and energy is a worth while investment.

Perception Can Be Deceptive

A point I always emphasize in my training sessions and lectures is this: *The closer the experience is to the expectation, the higher the satisfaction.* This is a cautionary statement designed to remind you that perceptions on one side of the table do not always match the perceptions held by persons on the other. You may think you have gone above and beyond in the offerings, but it may not appear that way to your customer or client. If you incorrectly assume the value your Nemesis assigns to what you have stacked on the table, you may sincerely feel you have given much, and the other side may feel you have given too little.

If, for example, your customer encounters a service problem with your product, and if you have thoroughly reviewed all materials in the customer service manual, you may surmise that as long as the product functions reasonably well, you have provided excellent service. Conversely, if the customer's expectations exceeded what you were able to offer, the customer may feel you provided poor service.

If you perceive a situation incorrectly, you could end up being the loser, not because of something you did or said but because you misread what was relayed to you. Words can be, and often are, confusing and can force you to forfeit goods or services you would prefer to keep. The best rule of thumb is to listen and analyze every situation carefully. Keep personal feelings intact, and try to SEE what the other person is really saying. Then and only then can you negotiate successfully.

Who Is President?

The following story illustrates this point. A friend of mine was vacationing with his family when his teenage daughter fell in a restaurant, hit her head, and cut her chin. She was taken to a hospital emergency room for a few stitches and a thorough check-over.

It soon became clear that the attending doctor was fairly certain there was no concussion or other serious damage. He applied stitches and dressed the wound.

As soon as he finished, the girl, who was obviously more composed and feeling better by this time, asked the doctor, "Can we go back to the hotel now?"

"I don't see any reason why not," he responded. Probably just to give himself final assurance that there was no hint of anything further needed, he added, half-jokingly, "Tell you what.   If you will answer three questions for me, I'll let your Dad take you out of here. What is your age?"

"Seventeen."

"Do you know where you are?"

"In the hospital."

"Who is our President?"

After a brief pause during which the young patient appeared somewhat confused and disoriented, she replied, "I don't know."

You can guess the doctor's response. "Why don't you just stay overnight with us and get some rest. We'll see about letting your Dad take you back to the hotel tomorrow morning."

As soon as the doctor stepped away to arrange admittance, my friend approached his high school senior honor student and asked, "Cynthia, why didn't you answer his question? You know good and well that Jimmy Carter is President of the United States." (This is an old story.)

"Oh, I thought he meant the president of the hospital," Cynthia said.

This example proves the point. It is vitally important when hunting for the best solution to know what the other side is thinking. Perhaps your Nemesis misunderstood a question. Probe deeply and clarify any vague issues.

When you identify what you can uniquely offer, you increase your assets at the negotiation table. Your uniqueness is the sum total of these assets. As we have discussed, the assets can take many forms. These items (assets) become your reserve arsenal even though you may or may not offer them. It depends entirely upon the situation. This approach, however, takes pressure off price, and price is far too often the lead topic of negotiation, far exceeding whatever comes in second at the negotiation table. Those who only negotiate price have just one negotiating tool—to lower the price. A Friendly Persuader packs the weapon case with more than the price tool.

Understanding what makes you unique (that is,

what you can offer other than price) increases your negotiating strength (that is, the strength that you have assembled while you were *inside the head* of your Negotiating Nemesis). These assets will be available to you as bargaining chips, increasing the chances that your Negotiating Nemesis will want to do business only with you.

If, however, you cannot identify what makes you unique, the only item left to negotiate is price. With price as your only target, you are really in trouble. Those who focus only on price, lose.

Conversely, when you know what is special about you, your service, your distribution, or other attributes, you have no competition. You will have revealed your uniqueness.

STEP FOUR: Ask for More Than You Want

I've known Mark Haroldson for more than twenty years. He has had phenomenal success in building a direct marketing empire. At the beginning of his career, he was a stockbroker who invested in real estate on the side. Mark later wrote a book about the tremendous growth of his net worth through his real estate investing, *Wake Up the Financial Genius in You.* That book and the added notoriety launched his highly successful seminar and educational instruction company. In these seminars, Mark first teaches real estate investing and later covers techniques involved in starting small at-home businesses.

In his early investing years, Mark bought and sold a piece of property. In the process, he helped finance the purchase for his new buyer.   This left him in possession of a note and deed of trust worth around $70,000.

Mark later received a call from a man who said he worked for the State of Utah. The caller's conversation was unbelievably revealing. He began, "I understand that you hold a mortgage on a certain piece of property. We're interested in paying off that note early because the government agency I represent is acquiring the property and planning to build a parking deck there. We are already in the condemnation process of acquiring the property. I am calling to see if you would be interested in giving us a discount for early payoff of the mortgage."

For any readers who are unfamiliar with the government's ability to take property under "the right of eminent domain," it simply means that under most circumstances, it can be done for the "common good" as long as the government gives just compensation. The government will offer the titleholder a low price but will always pay off the mortgage in full. Once the caller said the property was subject to condemnation, Mark knew he would be paid and had no reason to negotiate. I wonder how many people would have needlessly given the state a discount?

The Moral of This Story

You have to be very careful what you disclose in your negotiations. In this particular case, the government agent "spilled the beans" as my grandmother used to say. He not only told Mark that the note would be paid off early but in the same breath said it would be paid in full with or without a discount.

While there is only one Mark Haroldson, there are a number of other people who are equally astute. We must, however, give the Utah official credit. That call only cost the good citizens of Utah a few cents. The odds were greatly in his favor that he would not reach *the* Mark Haroldson. The odds were even greater in his favor that he would reach someone who was anxious to cash out of the note at a discount. Even though sloppy in his tactics, the government official applied one sound negotiation principle. He asked for more than he expected to receive.

There is one other lesson to be learned from this example. The Utah official made a crucial mistake. Did you detect it? He was not obligated to reveal, at least in the earliest stage of discussion, that he was acting on behalf of the state. He could merely have inquired as to whether or not Mark was interested in discounting the note. In this manner, he would have committed Mark to the transaction. From that point forward, the negotiation would simply center around working out the various details. It is likely that the net result would have been the State of Utah asking for something it didn't expect to receive but actually got — possibly even from one as astute as Mark Haroldson.

Have you ever made this mistake? Have you ever been too anxious or perhaps so nervous or even careless in making your presentation that you told the other party its advantage?

Be careful. Learn this lesson well. Never reveal your weakness and subtly reveal your strengths. As important, never tell the opposing team the advantage it has over you. With your strengths on the table, you will always make the best deal.

STEP FIVE: Never Say Never. Never Say No. Never Give In.

To paraphrase Winston Churchill: "Never, never surrender. Never give concessions." However, the prime minister wasn't buying a car or attempting to sell two fifty-yard-line tickets to a football game. Along with the rest of his fellow countrymen, he battled for his personal health and safety and for worldwide freedom. Always put the importance of the transaction in perspective. If you are negotiating for your life, there is one objective — to live. Most transactions we encounter on a day-to-day basis are less critical and better handled without a do-or-die attitude.

When negotiations reach the inevitable stage where both sides focus on money, it's time to introduce your newfound uniqueness. Focus on that uniqueness, then *trade-off.* By proposing a series of *trade-offs* — "I'll do this, if you'll do that" — you can successfully negotiate most deals.

In the following pages, I'm going to discuss a variety of proper negotiating procedures and the newly discovered Negotiating Paradox — how to get more by giving more. In so doing, you are going to find yourself going through an interesting metamorphosis.

As you read, a process of comprehension, association, and transition will begin to occur within you. (Just as it occurred with Dr. Frankenstein's infamous situation, a sure and certain charge will come over you.)

By the time you finish this book, you will have evolved into a true icon — not just another negotiator — but a Friendly Persuader.

5

The Toughest Negotiator You'll Ever Meet

There is a person out there who knows every move you make and the ones you are going to make in the future. This person knows why you offer the price you offer and can think faster than you can talk. You see this person in the mirror every morning. That's right. The toughest negotiator you will ever meet is you.

Yes, you heard me right. This information could be the classic good news/bad news. The good news is that you, my friend, are on the way to becoming a Friendly Persuader, and a Friendly Persuader would never allow the face in the mirror to become the Negotiating Nemesis. That trap is called *The Toughest Negotiator Syndrome.* Simply by being aware that this syndrome is a real trap, you will undoubtedly avoid falling into it. Yet, many have fallen prey.

By simply recognizing and acknowledging the face in the mirror and having knowledge of the rules, regulations, and pitfalls of this Syndrome, you will immediately spot it in others and be glad you are now immune to it.

Negotiating Against Yourself

To illustrate, I'll share a recent experience. My inventory manager told me we needed plastic page protectors. We had none in storage. Since sheet protectors are used to package supplies for one of our training courses, and since we had just received a large, first order from a new client who required immediate shipment, having no sheet protectors left us in a bit of a crisis. My manager asked me to meet him at a local office supply. He wanted my approval in case we needed to pick out an alternate item. We just didn't know if we would be able to purchase enough sheet protectors on such short notice since we generally ordered them for shipment in bulk.

At the office supply, we found what we needed. Although the box had been opened, our count revealed it held 100 covers. Happy to have enough sheet protectors, I said, "We'll take all of them."

The clerk immediately summoned the all-too-eager store manager who apparently appreciated our business. Without our asking, the clerk offered a ten-percent discount for the larger than usual order. Of course, we accepted.

Since we really needed a minimum of 200, we told her we needed a second box, so she dashed to the back storeroom and came out toting a second unwrapped box, proudly exclaiming, "You're in luck, and since your order is so large, I'll increase your discount to 15%."

Trying to please a customer, this zealous clerk failed to realize how desperately we needed these items. Premium price, sale price, made no difference. We simply wanted to purchase them all at once, get back to business, and ship our product. The alternative—running from store to store, picking up page protectors a dozen or so at a time—wasn't appealing and was counterproductive. Time means money. In light of our dilemma, I neither asked for nor expected a discount. When the store manager assembled the protectors, I noticed they were all similar but were different brands with an ever-so-slight color difference of white spine. Essentially the products were the same, were fully interchangeable, and were perfectly acceptable to us. I commented to my manager that the colors were slightly different. I really didn't care and was just thinking aloud—making an observation. I had no cause to complain. We had just solved an emergency supply problem.

Without hesitation, the manager said, "I'll give you another 2% off because of the color, but that's all I can do." Mind you, I hadn't asked for a discount. At this point, I was actually embarrassed because I had such a good deal.

The clerk again figured the price and totaled the sale. Although the extra discount was appreciated, it had nothing to do with my purchasing decision. To reduce my guilt, I decided to add to the purchase a few additional supplies which totaled about $15.

Placing the items on the counter, I asked the manger to include the additional merchandise on the bill. She promptly smiled and responded, "Too late. I already have it totaled. I guess these items are free. But, don't ask for anything else."

I was almost afraid to speak. You see, I knew the manager was negotiating against herself. She assumed that anyone who bought large quantities would demand the most competitive discount.

How to Beat the Toughest Negotiator Syndrome

I didn't complain, of course, but I could clearly see how much her negotiating cost her business. She wanted to make sure that a customer who purchased a larger-than-usual order was happy. To do so, she did what she thought would satisfy that customer. It was not necessary. She was negotiating against herself. Situations like this are common. Salespeople offer discounts or other things of value, thinking a discount will help close the deal.

How often have you felt like offering something extra to a buyer or seller, something you were sure your customers would consider valuable? You make these offers to keep on their good side, to make sure they are happy with the transaction, or to keep them coming back to you with their business. Yet, often your efforts are wasted. Unless your Negotiating Nemesis wants or needs what you're offering, you are throwing your money away. There is no excuse for not knowing what your Negotiating Nemesis wishes or needs prior to the negotiation. Without such knowledge, your negotiation efforts will be ineffectual. For example, if the office supply store manager had only asked a question or two about our requirements, something as simple as "Gosh, why do you need so many page protectors?" she would have understood that we needed her supplies more than she needed to offer a discount.

Silence Is Golden

Let's look at a powerful negotiating tactic that is

useful in similar situations. If you are in the role of the seller, this technique will prevent you from negotiating against yourself. If you are the buyer, it encourages your Negotiating Nemesis to offer you more. In a word—silence.

A personal example will help illustrate this point. While in my twenties, I continually worked on financially draining deals. (That was before I was old enough to learn to set limits, and I still thought all things were possible. Ah, the exuberance of youth.)

While working on an investment transaction worth five times my total net worth, I experienced a phenomenon familiar to many of you. I ran out of money. I needed some cash. Now, at the conclusion of an earlier transaction, I was left holding a rather large mortgage, almost $180,000.

Since I waited far too late to begin taking action, I resourcefully set out to solve my cash flow problem at breakneck speed, or as a friend of mine says, "Barney being in a hurry is like traveling at Mach II with your hair on fire." At any rate, I desperately needed cash. Amid my circle of friends (networking helps), I wound up with the name of a licensed note buyer in Santa Barbara who had two or three reliable investors lined up to fund his note purchases. I called, introduced myself, and explained my problem. Luckily, the investor responded favorably, saying, "Seems like an easy transaction and something we routinely do. My investors will pay around $130,000 to $140,000 for the note."

To complete the deal, I promptly furnished the investor with the necessary details and documentation. After viewing my package, the man assured me that he could easily close the deal with me. "When?" I asked.

It couldn't be soon enough.

"Probably Monday," he said.

Friday afternoon before the Monday we were to meet, I was as fidgety as a cat on a hot tin roof. Not wanting to pace the floor until Monday, I collected all the necessary papers. On Saturday, I caught a plane to Santa Barbara.

Sitting on that plane, I felt quite pleased at getting enough money to lift my financial burden, yet the big discount bothered me. Under normal circumstances, I probably would have declined the offer, but for now raising cash was imminently more important. The only other note buyer I knew (Marv Nieman in Denver) had offered me only fifty cents on the dollar. By comparison, the Santa Barbara offer looked really attractive.

Monday morning the note broker showed up at his office only to tell me that he had played golf with his doctor friend who had decided to "pass on this one." Did my heart stop beating? For a moment, I couldn't breathe. To add insult to injury, I had taken a cab to his office and had to walk, moping like some John Steinbeck character, to the nearest phone booth just to call a taxi to take me back to the hotel. Many of you can visualize the cloud of despair hanging over my head.

Before calling the taxi, I called Marv Nieman, the Denver broker, again, hoping almost beyond hope that he would offer additional money. To be honest, it wouldn't do me much good to sell so cheaply because Marv's offer didn't solve enough of my money problem to make much difference. I thought going for a second offer might prove fruitful. No such luck. In fact, when I said to Marv, "At that cheap price, you'll certainly give me an option to buy the note back for $95,000 or $96,000, won't you?", his reply was, "Option Smoption."

Marv certainly has a way with words. "If you have cash, I can find you a note. You can always find some note somewhere you can buy for fifty cents on the dollar. Why do you want your own note back?"

Logically, I had to agree, but the truth hurt. The truth was that anyone who was desperate enough to consider selling a note for fifty cents on the dollar was in no position to negotiate any additional terms or conditions. That's probably one of the first times in my life that I actually raised my arms up to heaven and tilted by head back and said, "I give up. Tell me what I should do."

Now, I know that some of you won't believe what I'm about to tell you, so if you prefer, you can simply chalk it up to Ol' Barney going slightly crazy, but I'll swear in court that a voice told me, "Call the person who's making the payments." Yes, it was a deep voice like out of a 1950's movie —you know the one when God spoke to Moses.

In thinking it over, calling made sense, and as it turned out this person seemed to be quite upset about being in debt. The note was secured by a building I had owned at 822 Figurora Street, downtown near the Hilton Hotel in Los Angeles, a prize piece of property to own especially for someone under age thirty. And, yes, you are right. I wish I still owned it today. My net worth would be a few million more, but at the time the note needed to be sold. Here I was again needing to sell this note.

I dialed the phone again, this time calling the building owner in Los Angeles. Starting with a somewhat garbled conversation, I asked, "Do you remember me? I'm the guy who sold you the building, and you owe me money secured by a note and a deed of trust."

"Yes," he replied.

"If you would be interested in paying that note off early, I'd be willing to take a small discount." I couldn't believe I was actually positioning myself for negotiating stature, standing there in a phone booth with the bulk of my cash reserves scattered on the shelf underneath the telephone.

"How much of a discount?"

Here's the critical part, folks. Those of you taking notes, write this down. I almost opened my mouth to name a number. In fact, with my excitement mounting at the prospect of settling this deal, it was no small miracle that I kept any control over my speech. Using the few seconds between words to calm myself, I said, "I don't know. What do you think is fair?"

"For a note of $180,000, you'd have to give me at least $5,000 to $10,000 off." My knees buckled as I almost fell out of the phone booth. Wanting to avoid stammering and trying to muster up my calmest voice, I said, "That would only be fair."

Sweat poured from my forehead. What a deal! And, yes, I did look up to the heavens and say, "Thank you, Sir."

It turns out that this gentleman had $100,000 available. A few days earlier, he had unexpectedly received money that was owed to him, and he was wondering what to do with his newfound wad of cash. I sold him the note for $100,000 cash and another note to be paid in sixty days for $70,000. He paid that in a timely manner to retire the debt. He was happy, and I was delirious.

This tight situation taught me a very solid lesson. Whenever possible, always let the other person start the negotiation process. If you say how high is high, don't you also set the limit on how low is low? When it is time for you to speak, make an offer that is very fair to you. Although it may be difficult, patiently wait for the other side to set the limits. While you remain silent, your Negotiating Nemesis must break the silence and speak.

He Who Talks First, Loses

In fact, silence is a vital ingredient in the negotiating process. The expression, "He who talks first, loses," is still true when you are asked a closing question. Ask your question, and then remain still and attentive. If you can wait longer than your Negotiating Nemesis, he or she may give in or at the very least tell you why a deal can't be made. Silence, as most of us know, is difficult. The truth is, some of us just have a tendency to talk too much.

An old story proves this point. A little girl stormed into the room and asked her dad where her little sister came from. The Dad, passing the buck, said, "Ask Mom." No luck.

The daughter asked again and then stood in silence. Attempting to provide a quick explanation, just hitting the high spots and leaving out as much detail as he possibly could, the girl's father started with a few details.

Not knowing where to quit, he went further and further, providing more and more detail. Soon, he felt totally embarrassed until his blabbering was met with stony silence from the daughter. Finally, he stopped talking and asked, "Did that answer your question?"

"No," the daughter replied. "All I wanted to know was which hospital she came from. I said it was the one downtown, where I was born, but she said the new one by the airport."

There's an old saying that I've used frequently: "Any faucet can turn the water on, but after a few years, only a good faucet will turn it off." The same principle applies to conversation. You can often prosper simply by being quiet.

Think about how you feel when someone fails to respond to you when you are trying to make either a purchase or sale. When the silence is deafening, most of us have the natural tendency to counter the silence by sweetening the offer.

Experienced negotiators fully understand that when a better offer is made and the offer doesn't receive an immediate positive response, the pattern will undoubtedly be repeated every time there is a hesitation in the conversation or when there is silence. Silence is uncomfortable for most of us. In reality, silence may simply mean the other person is thinking over the proposition or reviewing benefits.

Negotiating Pays

My friend Mark Haroldson once told me that his early real estate investments were successful because he had good negotiating skills. Since he wasn't formally trained in negotiating, he called it beginner's luck.

It is true that a few seem intuitively to understand the negotiating process, but most effective negotiators rely on some sort of training.

Mark's first meaningful investment, a small, 16-unit apartment, was structurally sound but in poor external condition. That was exactly the kind of property Mark sought—a building he could clean up and minimally fix up. Once repaired, such properties can be easily sold or recapitalized for a nice profit.

Being embarrassed with the low initial offer (approximately 60% of the asking price) he planned to make on the property, Mark put his bid in writing and dropped it by the owner's house to avoid a face-to-face meeting. A written response makes the offer seem more real while allowing the recipient time to read it several times. Other situations might require a softer handling. For example, a harsh offer might need to be explained before it can be placed in writing. But, in this instance, Mark's self proclaimed beginner's luck was right on target.

After a day had passed, Mark knew he would have to phone the seller for a response. After the initial hello, Mark introduced himself as the gentlemen who had offered the written bid.

Then , Mark made a wise move. He shut up to let the man respond. The first sentence out of the seller's mouth was, "Well, it looks pretty good to me, but there are a few details we have to work out." Mark said it was all he could do to keep an even tone and conceal the shock in his voice. This story is particularly pertinent to this book because it contains several rules related to the successful application and appreciation of the benefits of the Negotiating Paradox. You will find them repeated as you read.

Remember these points:

> *When you ask for what you want, ask for more than you expect to get.*

> *When you ask for it, be silent. Don't sit there and argue with yourself or try to justify your request.*

Give your Negotiating Nemesis a chance to say yes.

As difficult as silence may be, a Friendly Persuader must learn to use this listening tool. If you speak when you have already won, you may find that you unnecessarily stop the flow of additional benefits. If you as a seller keep talking, you never give the buyer a chance to say sold.

Sometimes it just pays to *shut up*. Let silence be one of your new secret negotiating weapons and watch out for the toughest negotiator, the one in the mirror. You want this tough negotiator on your side.

To sum up, remember this important negotiation rule, and never violate it: *NEVER negotiate against yourself.*

You negotiate against yourself when:

➢ *You attempt, sometimes too hastily, to sweeten the deal.*

You offer, say, $100 for a deal, and you are met with silence. That quiet time makes you nervous, so you say, "OK, make that $110." Your Negotiating Nemesis, whether knowingly or not, has just used the tool of silence.

➢ *You let your actions be prompted by a fear of losing a sale. Fear stifles your ability to negotiate effectively. Keep fear out of your life.*

➢ *You are the purchaser, and you are overcome by the fear that your Negotiating Nemesis will sell the product to someone else. "Want-ers" make bad negotiators.*

> *You reveal your level of need.*

Even if you're convinced that you must have a good or service and that if you don't possess it as your own, life will hardly be worth living, avoid letting your Nemesis know your desires or needs.

> *You get too anxious and offer a deal that is not particularly good for you when you can easily avoid such a deal. An anxious person winds up negotiating against the face in the mirror.*

Now that you have just come face to face with the toughest negotiator you will ever meet-*you*-this meeting should enable you to avoid the pitfalls of negotiating against yourself.

6
When You Can't Afford to Walk Away

A client once asked me, "How do you negotiate when you can't afford to lose the deal or walk away? How do you handle a union contract negotiation or demands from your biggest customer or the real estate deal you cannot afford to miss?" Don't let any of these frequent but important questions leave you in a quandary. If you find you are negotiating with a person or company who seemingly holds all the cards, you may fearfully think, "If I'm not careful, I'll lose my deal, my business, my job." Should you proceed cautiously or risk it all?

The answer is simple. Proceed cautiously. Plan carefully. Balance the scales. If you enter a negotiation believing you absolutely MUST win, you will ask for only what you feel your Negotiating Nemesis will surrender and nothing more. When you see yourself with few, if any, alternatives, you have moved from a creative Friendly Persuader to a passive observer. Your Negotiating Nemesis will dictate the terms, and they will definitely not be in your favor. In such a case, you will have already lost the negotiation.

Planning Pays

What should you do—give up? Maybe. Maybe not. Let's analyze the problem for alternative solutions. First, carefully plan negotiations. Very few people plan well enough. Some feel insecure when negotiating simply because they lack simple negotiations skills. Some foolishly think they do better ad-libbing or shooting from the hip. In reality, they will more than likely shoot themselves in the foot.

No one can skip the planning step. In this step, you decide precisely what you *want* to acquire in the negotiation, what you can *afford* to give away, and what you are *willing* to give away. You must define a range of benefits, prices, and terms, including the minimum you will accept. Maybe a good starting point would be to list and rank all the factors of your pending negotiation.

> ➢ *What factors are most important?*

> ➢ *What factors are least important?*

> ➢ *What are your real deadlines?*

> ➢ *What time frame absolutely won't work?*

> ➢ *Who's in charge?*

> ➢ *Who delivers?*

> ➢ *Who has the most input?*

Always draw the line on deal killers. That's right.

The line will be drawn somewhere. If you fail to draw it, the Negotiating Nemesis will, and you can rest assured that everything below the line will not belong to you.

Accept this fact: *There is no such thing as a negotiation from which you can't afford to walk away.* Without this option, you are not negotiating. You are surrendering.

At times, it may seem to you that you absolutely must keep a customer, go through with a deal, or agree to a contract — at any cost. Yet, effective negotiators are fully cognizant of times when the only way to win is to leave the negotiation without a signed deal. Factories close. Customers go elsewhere. Deals collapse. Most would agree that walking away may be a less than desirable solution, yet it must remain a choice.

Fortunately, for a trained negotiator, a Friendly Persuader like yourself, this step is seldom necessary.

Know Your Nemesis

The number of times you accept less than favorable terms or walk away from less than promising conditions can be reduced with careful planning. By studying your Negotiating Nemesis' history, you strengthen weak starting points and turn odds in your favor. You proceed by asking the right questions and following basic techniques. As you master these techniques, you will negotiate more successfully.

➢ *Know what your Negotiating Nemesis wants.*

➢ *Separate issues from personal feelings.*

➢ *Keep the momentum of the negotiation going.*

Since most negotiations are somewhat unbalanced, you can strengthen your position by reminding yourself that you have benefits your Nemesis desires. Why else would that person be negotiating with you? A Friendly Persuader knows the *real* wishes and needs of the Negotiating Nemesis — not just what the Negotiating Nemesis says they are. This rule applies to powerful labor unions, large and small corporations, and government agencies, as well as smaller firms. Standing alone, even large businesses would collapse. When companies are too demanding or inflexible, they risk suffering along with their competitors. Clearly, powerful companies can and have negotiated themselves right out of business.

PATCO

The Professional Air Traffic Controllers Organization (PATCO) strike in the early 1980s is a perfect example of an organization that negotiated itself out of business. PATCO made several mistakes in negotiating with the government to save the jobs of its air traffic controller members.

Relying on a rigid position and walking away too early, PATCO focused on its needs and was oblivious of what the government was prepared to enforce. When the government denied union demands, PATCO had one alternative: to leave the negotiation table. Look what happened. The union's take-it-or-leave-it approach forced many PATCO members to lose their jobs. Union leaders never believed that their members could or would be replaced. Surprise! Surprise!

Had the union negotiators more effectively assessed their opponent's position, they might have avoided boxing themselves into a tight corner. They underestimated what President Reagan would do. They assumed too much, and their assumptions were wrong. As an actor, Reagan had been an active union member, but he was now President of the United States of America. His perspectives had changed, and his duties and responsibilities now dictated that he consider a broader view of issues. PATCO members lost and lost big because union officials played hardball without thoroughly assessing the situation or considering alternatives available to their Negotiating Nemesis.

Concessions

A worthy Negotiating Nemesis generally has little concern for your costs, wants, or needs. He or she is primarily concerned with the potential overall benefits or prospects for personal gain. Don't be critical. A healthy, well-adjusted person protects personal interests. This situation, in fact, works to your advantage because it permits you to offer concessions that move you toward closure more quickly.

For example, closing dates, shipping terms, delivery dates, and financing can be valuable concessions very well worth many times their actual costs. If you are aware that your clients must close a transaction by a specific date or lose tax benefits, your agreement to close or deliver by that date may be worth thousands of dollars to them, though it doesn't cost you much, if anything.

The important point to remember is the value of some benefits far exceed their costs. You can only offer valuable concessions if you know what the other side needs or values. A Friendly Persuader always knows.

Separate Issues from Feelings

Besides being aware of the wants and needs of your Nemesis, you must be emotionally equipped to stay strong during the negotiation talks. Staying strong keeps you in the negotiation arena and helps avoid the *walking away* syndrome.

Untrained negotiators may have a tendency to become personally involved in interacting with a Negotiating Nemesis, taking each rejection or the terms of the proposal as a personal affront or rejection. Frustration can lead to anger. Anger often leads to blaming the Negotiating Nemesis for failing to reach a settlement.

Despite the opponent's actions, such disruptive behavior, personal accusations, or defamation rarely succeed. When such conditions surface, it is even more important to maintain a cordial personal relationship. Surprisingly, people can be rather accommodating when they successfully separate issues from personal feelings.

Arguments Cost You Deals

Once I had a problem with my phone bill. When I moved my office, the local phone company asked me to select a long distance carrier. I said, "Company XYZ," a small firm that resells phone service at a discount. XYZ was my previous carrier, and I was only moving four miles, so I expected no problems.

However, the local phone company could not find the

code for XYZ. I explained that XYZ was in the business of reselling long distance service it acquired from Company B, a well-known long distance provider that actually provided XYZ with phone line network and servicing.

The next thing I knew, a huge long distance bill from Company B was on my desk. I complained and asked for a correction, and I refused to pay the incorrect long distance charges.

Three months later (you guessed it) my phone service was going to be cut off for non-payment, and I was madder than a cat losing a prize mouse. My initial instinct was that I couldn't walk away from this deal. I needed my four business lines. I had become spoiled by XYZ, which only charged ten cents a minute and would break that up into six-second increments. My bill under Company B had tripled.

First, I did some quick research. I reviewed the federal laws on slamming, which is the practice by some phone companies of making you their customer without your permission. Unsure if that were the case or not, and in order to balance the scales in my favor, I planned to say slammed and slamming several times in my negotiations.

Carefully, I planned my attack. Since I absolutely needed local phone service, the local phone company and I had to remain friends. If I blamed them, the personnel would side with Company B.

I discovered another factor which really enhanced my position. It seems that a big long distance carrier had recently bought out my local phone company, Company C. Now, since Company B and Company C were head-on competitors, I decided that if I positioned myself along with the local phone company and Company C as the *good guys* against Company B, the *bad guys*, I could tilt the odds in my favor.

Satisfied in my decisions regarding my negotiating plan, I calmed down and rehearsed for my conversation with the local phone company. I needed to build an effective communication bridge with them. Anger tears down communication. After being referred to a customer service representative, Eddy, we chatted. Eddy later became my new best friend. She talked pure Texas, and that sweet accent certainly made the conversation much easier for me.

I asked her if all the new folks at Company C were as kind and understanding as she and all the other good folks at the local phone company were before Company C bought them out. We were bridged.

With Eddy on my side, I was ready to negotiate. I told Eddy of the mean old Company B. To help settle the dispute, Eddy called Company B for a conference call. We were both sure there was an easy solution.

When the lady from Company B picked up the phone, I was very firm. She got a little nasty. I did the talking initially, and Eddy stayed on the line to listen.

I informed the Company B lady that being nasty to me was fine, but she'd better not talk that way about my friend, Eddy, or Company C because they were just trying to solve my problem for me.

The lady from Company B got mean, and the conversation ended — again. I told Eddy the story and ended with, "See what I'm up against?"

Eddy and I talked about how we knew how to conduct business with tact and how it was too bad that other people couldn't conduct themselves properly. She then solved the problem, saying, "I'll just reverse all their charges for the last six months and block them from putting charges on your local bill." It was a done deal.

I thanked her profusely and found a new long distance carrier that afternoon.

Several lessons surface here. Learn them well.

> ➤ Plan your negotiations before you proceed.

This reinforces my earlier statement that most customer service activity is actually some form of negotiation. The woman from Company B blew the deal by making it an argument.

> ➤ Be yourself—just be your best self.

Everyone has personality traits that people admire. Keeping negative personal feelings away from the negotiation is vital to your success. Express negative reactions to proposed terms on a professional level.

> ➤ *Keep the momentum going.*

Once started, never let the negotiation stagnate or become delayed for extended periods.

> ➤ *Keep moving toward a closure.*

Take breaks or a recess, particularly if you reach an impasse, but keep the negotiating momentum intact.

> ➤ *If you must meet on another day, make it soon.*

As long as talking and meetings are ongoing, you are building rapport. These meetings allow you to learn a great deal about your Negotiating Nemesis. The more you know about your client or customer, the more likely you will move toward a close.

> ➤ *Learn your client's or customer's needs.*

Remember, ask, and listen.

> ➤ *Stay firm and focused as you close the transaction.*

Always keep the negotiation pointed toward the closing.

> ➤ Decide precisely what you want and what you can afford to give away.

You must define a range of benefits, prices, and terms, including the minimum you will accept.

> ➤ Acknowledge the fact that you can afford to walk away from any negotiation deal.

Without this option, you are not negotiating — you are merely accepting the terms dictated by your Negotiating Nemesis, and you are accepting them in slow, bitter stages.

> ➤ Instead of walking away or giving up more than you need to concede, try keeping personal feelings out of the negotiation and focus on issues and solutions.

Keep your emotions in check. Remember, it is not so much *you* against *him or her*, as it is *your position* against *his or her position*. This is, after all, a negotiation, not a personal confrontation. When you focus on the issues, you are also forcing your Negotiating Nemesis to do likewise, whether the person intends to or not.

> *Know what you are willing to offer and persevere.*

If you have done everything you can and the deal remains outside the limits you have defined and arbitrarily set for yourself, then walk away.

Walking away may be the best way to win.

7

But They Only Want to Talk Price

"There is hardly anything in the world that someone cannot make a little worse and sell a little cheaper. And, the people who consider price alone are this man's lawful prey."

Although John Ruskin made that statement a century ago, several quality-oriented and successful companies use that slogan today. Poorly trained or untrained sales personnel and even some top executives, however, cling to the notion that if they could just get a little more leeway on price from their bosses, they could close any deal. They more than likely are right, yet such thinking can be flawed.

I well remember the caption of a cartoon on the wall of a retail store I owned in the early 1960s: "I always bought my supplies for less than that, down the street at Joe's, until he went busted."

More than humorous, the cartoon message demonstrates that while a lower price may increase sales, if the price is low enough, you can sell yourself right out of business. A salesperson who always has the lowest price on a product or service is an *order taker*, not a salesperson. It is not possible to make up losses by increasing volume.

I am reminded of the shirt salesman who lost fifty cents on each shirt he sold, but he was doing a whirlwind business. He thought he could make it up on volume.

If the lowest price ever equated to automatic success, the marketplace would consist only of Hyundais and K-Marts. The Mercedes-Benz and Neiman-Marcus realm of the world would have to close its doors.

Highlight Your Benefits

While giving workshops and seminars to top executives and marketing specialists of major corporations, I generally ask the question, "How many of you have ever bought a Yugo?"

In the midst of mild amusement, the response to the question is usually the same. Practically no one bought a Yugo. Furthermore, most indicate that no one in their extended families ever owned one either.

"Why not?" I asked. "At the time the Yugo was marketed, it was the least expensive car you could buy, and it was actually marketed as such." One response was that the Yugo was made out of recycled Yugoslavian beer cans. Another answered that the Yugo was the only car that would double in value with a full tank of gas.

Such comments are striking validation of my point that price isn't everything. If people were only interested in price when buying a car, the Yugo would have sold millions. But, commercially, the Yugo was a flop.

It is obvious that other things such as reliability, reputation, style, and pride of ownership play more important roles. Successful companies realize that cutting price to the bone does little to increase sales unless customers need or want their services. More importantly, these same companies have found that customers shop for value, so providing more value than your competition is often the answer.

People naturally focus on price because dollars and cents are specific, tangible commodities that make comparisons easy. If you buy or sell a house, you naturally want to share the excitement of your bargain with relatives and friends. You tell them you got a *great* price. When receiving large discounts on personal items, you may share your department store victories.

However, when making a serious investment or negotiating commercial or industrial purchases, much more than price falls on the table.

Adding Value

Value, as you can see, makes the entire deal bigger. To make the deal bigger, you must put more elements in the deals that are negotiable and carefully point out those advantages to the other side. By doing so, you bring value to the negotiation table.

What is there in value? If you're arguing over price and you happen to be the highest quality producer in a business, the other person may be taking high quality for granted. To make the sale, you need to highlight that point.

Once when purchasing a car, I had a salesperson focus too much on price. Since I always think the asking price of a new car is too high, we immediately started haggling over (and it *was* haggling) the price. The salesperson left nothing else for us to discuss.

I later visited another dealership and was offered the same car at approximately the same price. This smart Friendly Persuader at the second dealership took the time to show me how buying from his dealership was superior to buying from any other dealership. This person pointed out the company's faster delivery time, longer reputation in business (therefore they were more trustworthy), and better financing. It made perfect sense, and I bought the car from them.

We all know that to make any deal bigger, you can just expand in volume and unit size, and you will correspondingly expand in dollars and gross. You can also make the deal bigger and expand your negotiating power and ability by being able to identify all the facets and all the quantitative factors besides dollars and cents and units. You do this, of course, by asking questions and having thorough knowledge of your products.

Remember that value is relative to a person's perception. You can only *offer* value if you know what your *customer values* or thinks is important. If, in addition, you add items or customize the product in some way, you can increase your product's value in the eyes of the customer.

This is the *perception* of which we've been speaking. If your client or customer wants pizza with extra cheese, give that person pizza with extra cheese. Your customer will return to you time and again.

Amateurs Concentrate on Price

The tangible success of some Friendly Persuaders separates them from amateurs who concentrate solely on price. Talking price is easy.

A Friendly Persuader penetrates price barriers and confidently discusses value and many other factors, always highlighting those as benefits to the Negotiating Nemesis. When confronted by a Negotiating Nemesis who keeps hammering price, you, as a Friendly Persuader, can smile internally in the knowledge that you *have* your Nemesis. You will win with your prepared dissertation of truly important factors. You can clearly and significantly show how your item is superior to all other products in the category. If the item is only slightly better than the competition's, you focus on a benefit your competitors failed to stress.

With this simple technique, you will increase your bottom line, and your Negotiating Nemesis will get the deserved quality.

Adding Value Is Easy

Once when I put together a series of education tapes for a company, I went to one supplier and had them produce the first set of 5,000 copies. Another supplier called me and said, "We'll not only produce the set, but we'll package it specifically for you. And, we have custom delivery." This supplier went on to point out these benefits in detail. I naturally switched suppliers.

My former supplier later called and wanted to know why I had switched. I told him I had received all those additional things at the very same price from another place. They said, "Gee, if you had asked me for these things, I would have added them in, and I wouldn't have lost your business." I thought, "How sad." If my first supplier had only taken the time to find out I had those wants or needs, I wouldn't have *HAD* to change suppliers. Always keep in mind that it is not up to your customers to find out what is available. It's up to you to let them know.

When Price Doesn't Count

An easy way to put price into perspective is to pose the hypothetical question: If you or a family member required a heart transplant or other serious surgery, would you shop for the lowest-price surgeon? Of course not. You would undoubtedly proclaim, "I want the best." Some people will even say, "Get me the most expensive surgeon you can find." If you were on trial for your life, would you select the cheapest attorney? Unlikely. You might even take pride in telling people your attorney is the most expensive one around.

Of course, these life-threatening situations are different from most day-to-day negotiations. Each case rests on a clearly defined objective. *Save my life — whatever the cost.* A serious event poses little need for debate. Saving your life is a clear objective, yet in other, less critical circumstances (such as renewing last year's contract with your largest customer or closing the sale on a warehouse), the objective may be more difficult to identify. Since people buy goods and products for different reasons, objectives will always vary from negotiation to negotiation and from person to person.

Know Your Buyer's Motivation

Some buyers buy in order to feel good. Purchasing agents feel secure when they make the best decisions for their company. The bonuses they receive don't hurt them either. They often take great pride in being able to obtain for the company the best deal.

These buyers buy in part for emotional reasons, and perhaps emotional reasons play a larger role than most of us normally think. Although buyers talk price and rationalize their decision making process, the reality is that they usually make purchases or sign contracts in order to satisfy psychological, emotional, or physical needs.

Ask Questions

To best identify concerns, needs, and desires of your customer or Negotiating Nemesis, you must ask these questions.

➢ *Is the Negotiating Nemesis one who buys only from a friend?*

➢ *Does the Negotiating Nemesis demand reliability more than anything else?*

➢ *Is value weighted more heavily than other options?*

➢ *Is value placed on a long-term supplier commitment?*

➢ *Does the customer value technical assistance?*

➢ *Is fast delivery an important concern?*

➢ *Is trying to "look good" to the boss of prime consideration?*

➢ *Does the company place higher concern on extended*

terms, and is it willing to pay more for improved cash flow?

Almost any one of these considerations can outweigh price if your Negotiating Nemesis needs it and if you are prepared to offer it.

Even the federal government, which uses a lowest-bid purchasing system, must by law consider the reliability of the bidding company and how closely the products or services offered in the bid match the government's need.

Controversy exists over such practices. When the defense department purchases military planes and weapons, they must also purchase the manufacturer's product warranty at an additional cost. Manufacturers, though, are rarely asked by the defense department to honor these warranties and, therefore, seldom pay a dime.

In reality, the warranties were often more profitable to manufacturers than were production and delivery of the actual weapon or airplane. So, why buy the warranty? Because it is often a federal requirement.

The Friendly Persuader representing the successful defense manufacturer knew this policy and factored the cost into the bidding process. If making a buying decision based only on the lowest bid isn't satisfactory for Uncle Sam, then it's not going to be good enough for your buyers either.

Customers Buy for Benefits

When we first upgraded our company to the computer age, we, like most companies, were faced with the challenge of deciding which computer to buy and which software to use.   To assess the situation, we requested quotes or bids.

When the time came to pick a vendor, we chose one that had an accessory the others lacked, but which we oh-so-desperately needed, even though that system cost us a few hundred dollars extra. That accessory was Tommy.

Tommy was the technician on call who would repair, replace, fix, or do whatever we needed on short notice to keep the system going. As it turned out, we only needed him once during the first year, but I can assure you that we were thankful we had Tommy.   The extra upfront money came back many times over when an employee pushed the wrong key and crashed the system.

Of course, this mishap occurred during a most critical project. Without immediate technical assistance, we would have been stuck. We paid for truly dependable service, and that benefit turned out to be a financially rewarding investment.

Benefits, Values, and Generic Brands

If you stop and read a couple of generic brand labels, you will find that they usually have essentially the same ingredients as do their name-brand cousins. With a bit of research, you will discover that many of your favorite name brands manufacturers actually produce or package the generic brands. Typically, the product in the generic can is the very same, yet it sells for less than its name-brand sibling. Then, why aren't generic products runaway best sellers? Let's face it, consumers feel uncomfortable with generic brands. Is the product *really* the same?   Does it look the same?

Does it taste the same? Does it have the same texture? What about size and color? I don't want my green beans cut up funny. Will that peanut butter stick to the roof of my kid's mouth? Does it have more fat? Less nutrition?

I've watched people read both familiar and generic-brand labels and, out of preprogramed faith, pick the higher price product over and over again. Since consumers have learned to trust the name brand for value, they generally overlook the cheaper brand and willingly, it seems, pay a higher price.

I've been told that talcum powder (name brand *and* generic) for practically all West Coast sellers is manufactured at one plant. Yet, the introduction of a generic talcum powder was a monumental flop.

I can tell you that Moms out there are picky. What loving Mom wants to be known, even by a check-out clerk, as someone who uses cheap (and possibly inferior) stuff on her child? Dads aren't much better at evaluating generic brands either. With Moms and Dads running the show, generic talcum powder didn't stand a chance.

A Benefit-Oriented Sales Pitch

Since benefits have strong consumer and company appeal, you should find a straightforward way to point out your every conceivable benefit to your Negotiating Nemesis. This is no time to be humble. A *benefit-oriented* sales pitch is more effective than a thousand word *feature-oriented* sales pitch. First, you turn features into benefits. Then, you make the sale.

Let me illustrate the difference between a feature and a benefit. A vacuum cleaner is often an upright piece of equipment. One end has brushes. The handle is about four feet long. The color is often gray, burgundy, or hunter green—depending on whatever is fashionable at the time.

A vacuum cleaner is a specific-use instrument, but it has many varied *potential* benefits. The machine cleans dog and cat hair off the couch. It sucks peanut hulls off the floor. It gets dirt out of the rug, is lightweight, and will last a long time. The tough plastic exterior will endure knocks and scrapes.

Shoppers look for these and other benefits when purchasing a vacuum cleaner. Value is, of course, always a benefit.

Customers look for something that makes the product more desirable or better suited to their needs. The vacuum cleaner that has all the standard benefits and, as a bonus, has an extra long cord to reach from room to room has added value for many homeowners. After all, who wants to plug and unplug the vacuum cleaner every time a new room is cleaned?

A smart manufacturer who has installed a longer cord as standard equipment on a machine will point out *that* added feature on the front of the package. This feature adds value.

Informed customers will weigh all options and pick the product that is most valuable to them. This will usually be the product with the most added value.

Every product, service, piece of equipment, or investment has special features that provide unique benefits that, in turn, equate to value. It is the mission of the Friendly Persuader to find all added values and then highlight them to make certain that the Negotiating Nemesis hasn't missed them.

Keep in mind, too, that benefits are not everything.

If you determine that your Negotiating Nemesis is buying, for example, for emotional reasons, then you must highlight the benefits that you believe to be relative to your client's or customer's emotional need.

For example, if you have reason to believe that Mom wants peanut butter with a certain picture on the label and your brand doesn't have the picture, then you had better find a way to attach the picture on your label. Otherwise, Mom will just attach her emotions to the competitor's peanut butter.

It all comes down to a balancing act, a game of sorts, but it is a serious and honest game, nonetheless. And, it is a game you must play to win.

Balancing the Teeter-Totter

To get a clearer understanding of the process, consider the teeter-totter board from the children's playground. For a playground teeter-totter board to be perfectly balanced, there must be equal weight on each side of the fulcrum.

Envision that on a business teeter-totter, a potential seller has weighed one side with price but has secretly attached helium balloons, called *features and benefits,* to the end of the board. The buyer has weighed the opposite end with obstacles to the seller's price and has attached hidden helium balloons labeled *real and emotional needs.* To balance the board, each side must consider the opposing obstacles negatively. Each side must view all obstacles, for example, as *lack of value* or *absence of service.* Each party to the negotiation will usually attach a long list.

When negotiations open, the buyer perceives that the seller is sitting high in the air holding the product, and the buyer's end of the board is touching the ground, loaded down with the burden of objections to overcome. Meanwhile, the price, which is still unknown, is *sky-high* or literally as high as it can be.

For every obstacle the buyer can remove, the price will come down. As a result, with every objection the seller can counter by keeping the would-be obstacle on the board, the seller can focus on items other than price. You can readily see that this process is likely to reach a conclusion where the price is commensurate with obstacles (value).

Now, from the seller's viewpoint, the buyer is up in the air — quite literally. While the seller sits on the ground with solid value, the seller's job is to push that value to the other side of the teeter-totter to balance the equation. The smart seller, knowing there are a limited number of chances, begins to ask probing questions while remaining very observant.

Once the right "needs" are discovered, and once the true "objections" (real and imaginary) are revealed, the seller begins moving the necessary information to the other side of the board. That information might be a benefit. It might be an appeal to emotions. It might be a solution to a problem. It might be something as simple as a smile. It might be a warranty, faster service, or less shipping costs. In actuality, it could be a thousand things. A Friendly Persuader has carefully analyzed the situation and knows when to push items and when not to push.

Sears Sells the Brand Name

Remember the movie, *Tin Man?* Just as it was with the tin man in the movie who was traditionally positioned at or near the lowest rung on the ladder of credibility, many people assume that precautions should be taken when doing business with aluminum siding sales personnel.

Prospective buyers are watchful, often believing that these salespersons are out to get them to sign up for something they don't want and frequently don't get, even when they pay for it.

One reputable installer I knew told me that most of his siding installation business came through Sears. I was surprised.

"Sears sells siding, but Sears doesn't install it," he replied. "My crews apply it. We do the contracts. It's the same siding that we sell and install under our own contracts or sell through Apcoa or A Best or one of the other siding companies."

"Do you make as much money when Sears makes the sale for you?" I inquired.

"No." He replied. "Sears takes a big profit chunk off the top, yet people call Sears because they know the Sears name. They know that they can trust Sears, and they are afraid of being taken by *the siding man*. We come out with the same truck that we always use, but I put a magnetic 'Sears Siding' sign over our sign before we go out on a Sears job."

The bottom line—Sears is not selling siding. Sears is selling the reliability and trustworthiness of the Sears' name. Sears takes the order, invoices the sale, and makes a nice profit. The siding is estimated, delivered, and installed by a *tin man*, often with a temporary Sears sign on his truck.

There's nothing wrong with this arrangement. Everyone is satisfied. American capitalism has never been better.

Be a Brand Name

Would you like the power of being a brand name? Being able to list how your firm or operation is different from the competition will move you in that direction. Brand names stand for *something*, but not *everything*. In mustard it's French's or Grey Poupon. In recliners it's Lazy Boy.

And, for how many years have you referred to your office copier as "the Xerox machine" when actually its manufacturer's label starts with an 'S" or a "C" or some such letter? Some folks simply have the quality name captured. In the Barney Dictionary, you will find that under "name-brand over-recognition."

What connotation does your company express to an observer? The first step in making this determination is to know why your customers seek your services.

Al Babzar, a consultant and trainer with in-depth experience in the heating and air-conditioning arena, shares how company owners learned a dramatic lesson about their customers. In advance of a training seminar, Al instructed his attendees to bring a sampling of customer invoices with them.

During the meeting, Ed was the first selected to join Al on the stage. Al leafed through Ed's most recent invoices, asking him, one by one, why he thought each customer had bought from his company. Ed was certain that a heavy majority of his customers bought from him based on price.

Al produced a speakerphone, selected one of the invoices, and asked Ed to call the customer.

"Call someone whom you think buys from you because you offer a lower price," Al said. Ed dialed Mr. Johnson's number.

Mr. Johnson, the customer, answered the phone. Al explained that he was conducting an industry survey of recent equipment buyers and asked if Mr. Johnson would mind telling why he picked Ed's company as his supplier.

Mr. Johnson said, "I'm in my late 70s. I may not be around here much longer, and I wanted a company that would be in business after I'm gone. That way my wife could call the company that sold us the unit if she had problems." Mr. Johnson continued, "I happen to know that Ed is one of four brothers who took over the company from their dad. I figured there were pretty good odds one of them would still be around in ten years or so if they were needed."

Just to double check, Al asked Mr. Johnson, "What about price?"

Mr. Johnson replied, "Ed wasn't the cheapest, but he was competitive." Mr. Johnson added, "As a matter of fact, I checked on the cheapest supplier just the other day, and you know what? They've already gone out of business."

There are two valuable lessons in this story. How can you be a strong negotiator without knowing why your clients buy from you? Your core presentations could be based on faulty assumptions.

And, as you'll hear me say over and over again, most of us are guilty of erroneously placing too much emphasis on price, believing that price is what buyers focus on first. Price plays a much smaller role than most buyers think.

Let's take a moment to explore some features and benefits that could be especially attractive or desirable to your potential clients or customers. Review this list from time to time. Eventually, these concepts will become part of the natural way you execute your sales pitch.

> ➤ *Look at company experience.*

If your company has been around for twenty-five, fifty, or seventy-five years, you should certainly make your existing and potential customers aware of it. Many buyers base purchasing decisions on the experience of a supplier.

> ➤ *It is seldom enough to simply state the feature. You must turn each feature into a benefit that your Negotiating Nemesis can understand and appreciate.*

Avoid assuming that the other side knows how features such as twenty-five years in business can be a benefit with real added value. Always remember that twenty-five years of experience helps you save time (because you've done this before) and reduces the chance of repeating the errors that a competitor with less experience is sure to make. Experience is a powerful teacher.

> ➤ *Remember to include in your sales presentation both the features and the benefits of several points. Then, summarize your sales presentation by relisting them.*

This technique hammers the point home and helps make your list of benefits longer and more valuable.

> ➤ *Since customers generally consider suppliers who are nearby, a convenient location is important.*

If you are located close to your customer, point that out. Otherwise, don't mention it. Keep the focus on your assets. People, on the whole, want to know how you can help them.

➢ *Name recognition, if you have it, is important.*

As illustrated in the aluminum siding example, customers worry less with a name they know and trust. Be sure to establish your reputation for quality in the community and, over time, you will build up your name recognition in a positive way.

➢ *Customers place a premium on service.*

Regardless of what your *product* is, service is always important. If your product is conducive to delivery, always provide delivery service as part of your offerings. I am always amazed at the *value premium* most consumers place on something as simple and easy as delivery.

➢ *Reliability is important.*

In addition to the delivery of your product, always, always deliver on what you promise. Accept that your customer expects your product and service to be exactly as he or she understood you to represent it.

It is a mistake to offer faulty products or services. Customers want products that work. In fact, an executive recently said to me, "The most expensive machine that we can buy is the one that doesn't work. Regardless of how much we pay for it, that is the most expensive one." So, provide quality goods and services if you expect return business.   Otherwise, you will soon be out of business with little hope of getting anyone's trust again.

> *Ease of use is also valuable to consumers.*

This certainly applies today when we talk about computers and software. The term "user friendly" has gained even wider application than ever, thanks to the high tech explosion in the 1990s.

> *Make sure you are represented by friendly and courteous people.*

This is one of my personal value leaders when elaborating the features and benefits of products and services to customers or potential clients. I would rather deal with someone who is friendly and easy to work with than the alternative anytime. I'm willing to bet you would, too. This is another of those times and instances when, if you have friendly and helpful personnel, you should make sure that you proudly point this out in your presentation. Your potential client will give it extreme value.

The people within an organization have value as individuals. People revisit stores where employees are friendly and fair. If you can't boast of this asset, then you should keep silent about your personnel. Following the presentation, go back to your shop, store, or office and do something about it before your next presentation.

Stealing Business

Have you ever heard of a salesperson leaving a

company and taking a *chunk* of business?

My barber, Danny, experienced this *stealing* of a business first hand. Two of Danny's barbers talked the landlord into evicting Danny so they could own the shop in partnership with the landlord. Their plan backfired. Danny was forced, by the landlord on a technicality, to vacate his shop, but soon his old clients found his new location. The sabotaging former employees and their partner (the landlord) are still struggling to survive in the business. Serves them right.

Never underestimate your value. If you're in sales, respect your own talents and abilities. Remind your Negotiating Nemesis that one reason for doing business with your firm is that you will personally follow through on what was negotiated.

If you have properly "sold" the other party on your ability, then you have an added benefit of real value that you have offered in the deal.

Differentiate

By pointing out benefits to consumers, you show differences between your product or service and the product or service of others. As you can see, the ways to differentiate products are endless. If you don't differentiate, then you have nothing special to offer or sell.

A perfect example of this involves the Singer company. Mr. Singer invented the sewing machine a hundred years ago. For years and years, there were forty or so brands of sewing machines on the market. Singer made about thirty-two of them.

For marketing purposes, Singer used private labels on these machines. Because of the way the machines were marketed, buyers had different perceptions of what they were buying. Virtually all the internal parts were Singer, but Singer's strategy allowed customers to purchase in accordance with what they valued the most. This technique has now become a common practice among manufacturers. Knowing these strategies and being aware of when to use them to your advantange will enable you to succeed more often when at the Negotiating scene.

Focus on Benefits

When you focus on benefits that your buyer wants or needs, you are, at the same time and as an added benefit to you, keeping that person's mind off price. Informed, aggressive, and ambitious buyers will always try to get a large price concession from you. Usually this technique is nothing more than a negotiating ploy (maybe the only one they know), and they ultimately pay more than they initially suggest to you as being their top price.

The Negotiating Nemesis rightfully figures price reductions are worth a try, and sometimes it works. You, however, as a Friendly Persuader, will know it if the lowball offer is unrealistic because you will know the market. Also, you won't be taken in by the "You'll have to do better than that" negotiation ploy, either.

When this question is posed to you, always ask, "How much better?" Then, when you are given an answer, ask for a concession in return. Remember that your Negotiating Nemesis is trying to do what is best for his or her company. Watch out for these price-cutting techniques.

Foremost in keeping your price intact is to have a printed price list or agreement readily available. It is psychologically more difficult to question printed authority even if you seldom or even NEVER expect to sell anything at the price you have printed. Your printed price will automatically appear less negotiable than verbal quotes.

Product Uniqueness

Before you can support and defend your price, you have to know your product's unique features and be able to translate those features into customer benefits. Whether you're selling goods, services, or property, you have a product and that product has unique features. Few, if any, products are the same, despite similar internal contents. The same item delivered sooner or from a more reliable company is a different product, and you point this out in your discussion of benefits and features. Always remember to tailor the description of your product to match the needs of your Negotiating Nemesis.

Other examples of unique features include:

> *Payment terms*

> *Guarantees*

> *Service*

> *Management (for property)*

> *Custom specifications or labels*

It always surprises me how hard some companies try to sell something other than what the customer wants. They further compound the error in thinking that price is the obstacle that prevents them from closing the deal. Remember that you can't sell buyers apples if they want oranges, even if you are offering apples at a big discount. The customer has to want what you have to offer. Otherwise, you are pushing the wrong product to the wrong client or customer. Line up your product with the right consumer to make the sale. This strategy will save you time, frustration, and money.

Negotiate Price Concessions

If your buyer really wants a price concession, you have to decide if you can grant it and still survive. Only then can you move to the less serious question of whether or not you are better off making the sale at the reduced price or simply walking away from the deal and selling your product elsewhere.

Once I was negotiating the sale of training courses with a potential client, an international distributor. He told me that he had reviewed my printed price list and had found a price he liked. Yet, I was still unable to close the sale. We had listed several prices based upon quantity. In this case, the quantity required for the price he liked exceeded the customer's need. When we learned what the problem was, we quickly agreed to give the lower price and accept a split order — one shipped now, another in ninety days.

The combination order totaled the quantity level that our list required. With this technique, we were able to give the price that our customer wanted to pay. This simple negotiation enabled us to maintain the integrity of our pricing structure, and the buyer was happy since he received the desired price.

If possible, any pricing schedule should use a graduated scale, a practice that will allow you to give a price concession without giving a price reduction in order that you can obtain a large order.

Another way to satisfy the price sensitive buyer is to offer a discount for cash payment on delivery. Cash flow has value to you, too.

Sometimes, without compromising product quality, you can change the specifications of the product to meet a customer's lower price needs. For example, we offer half-day seminars for companies when they are unable to afford the standard one-day presentation within their budget constraints. Always be cautious, though, and avoid making a unilateral price concession without receiving some *trade-off* from your customer. Without concessions, your customer may feel the original price was inflated or unfair in the first place and is likely to be more cautious in dealing with you in the future.

This is also another tactic that you can use in order to move negotiations away from the concentration on price. If your Negotiating Nemesis likes what you have but wants a better price, say, "Sure, we can offer that price. We'll just remove . . . ." Then, you should actually *take away* an important ingredient from the negotiating table. Naturally, your Negotiating Nemesis will, in turn, object. You, then, can return to your original offer.

The object of this exercise is to determine how important price really is to your Nemesis or whether he or she is just trying to hammer you down to the lowest possible price.

If skillfully handled, you avoid undesirable discounts while you appear to be most accommodating. You definitely can't be accused of refusing to negotiate.

Raise the Floor of the Price Range

Finally, here is a tip specifically for sales and marketing managers. Salespeople will zealously defend a price if they believe it to be the lowest possible price they can offer. Experience and observation have proven that when given a range of acceptable prices, salespeople are most comfortable when they quote their customers a price just above the minimum authorized. I have found that this range is somewhere around twenty percent above the minimum. A salesperson with the authority to do so who is given a range of $70 to $90 will aim at $75 to $77 as a fair price for the product or service but if cornered will go to $72. If given a range of $80 to $100, the salesperson will focus on $86 to $88 and put the bottom at $84. As you can see, the message is clear. Raise the minimum.

Raising the floor of the price range is an easy way to increase profitability and maintain pricing structure. All you're really doing is tightening your original sales range to a spread you really expected to sell within in the first place.

To enhance this technique further, some companies have special product cost information for their sales staff. If you are a buyer, just remember that fixed prices are usually not as fixed as the seller implies. This concept is somewhat true but with a different wrinkle, whether you're the buyer or seller.

Either way, as a Friendly Persuader, you'll frequently be able to use this knowledge to your advantage. The profits to you and your company can be protected. It is and always will be your job to protect yourself and your company. That is the only way to stay in business.

When Buyers Talk Price

The next time your buyers only want to talk price, listen attentively. Find out what they value besides price. If they aren't talking, ask them questions.

Remember, above all, if I'm your Negotiating Nemesis, and your only sales pitch is price, then the only reason I will buy your product is because it is cheap.

8
The Critical but Forgotten Step

In life, all too many people who are poorly trained in the art of negotiation may plan for a negotiation session (and planning certainly pays) and they might even ask relevant questions to determine exactly what their Negotiating Nemesis wants. Nevertheless, an often forgotten aspect of the overall negotiation process is the *trade-off.* This critical step brings the most valuable commodity to the negotiating table — satisfaction. For the transaction to be considered successful, you *and* your Negotiation Nemesis must leave the table satisfied.

Selling Too Cheap

Suppose you list your house for sale at $200,000. Realistically, you are hoping to get something in the $190,000 price range. If a couple views the home for just a moment and without haggling offers a cashier's check for the full amount, how would you feel? Happy? Probably not. Think about it. It is a natural reaction for you to feel that something wasn't right or that you could have gotten more. You and your spouse would probably excuse yourselves and, when out of earshot, say, "Oh, oh! We sold too cheaply." Then, inevitably, one of you would add something like, "Do you think we can tell them the price doesn't include the roof?"

That empty feeling occurs because there was no exchange, no process of negotiation. The key point is that although you received your full asking price, you feel less than satisfied.

Of course, it's always possible that the couple just won the lottery or inherited bizillions of dollars and money doesn't mean anything to them. It's also possible that they were just foolish — or didn't care.

However, in real life, we can't expect or even hope to encounter less-than-adequate adversaries in our Negotiating Nemesis. It's not likely that would have been the case in this example either. Admit it. You sold the house too cheaply. It was underpriced. Why did it happen? Because you, the sellers, failed to research the market properly. The result was leaving money "on the table." The house could have been sold for more. Always remember you can reduce the price but can never raise it. A higher price leaves room for a *trade-off* until all parties are satisfied.

When you allow for a *trade-off*, you allocate room to come down with a carefully timed, "O.K., I'll come down $5,000 in exchange for a quick close" (or something else of benefit to you).

Let's look at another scenario for the same sale. The potential buyers, after seeing the house, offer $192,000. You counter their offer with $195,000. They conditionally accept, asking you to pay for title insurance. Finally, you agree. The exchange is challenging, and you receive a fair price, $195,000 on a $200,000 asking price. Plus, you feel better than you felt in the first situation, although you settled for less money. The latter brings satisfaction.

It's important to recognize that people negotiate to feel good about the results, not just to minimize or maximize the dollars spent or received. In our second example, less money resulted in more satisfaction.

Never Give Anything Away

If there is a single rule to improve the success of your negotiations, it would be to never give anything away. Always made a trade. Don't give up anything without requesting something in return. Not only will you conclude the negotiation in a better position, but your buyer's (or your seller's) satisfaction automatically increases as well.

For example, how would you have felt if you had asked for a lower price the last time you purchased supplies or visited a doctor's office, and you received it? If the seller drops the price without hesitation, you may deem the original price as unfair and would, undoubtedly, feel you would have been cheated if you had neglected to ask for a reduction.

Likewise, if you offer a unilateral concession, your customers have every right to believe you attempted to elevate the price. Haven't you given them proof? They may very well analyze the situation from a negative point of view, thinking, "Huh? I wonder how often I've been overcharged in the past because I didn't insist on a discount?"

Such thinking can occur even if your intent is for the discount to be a gesture of goodwill. A request for a concession that is met with an offer for a *trade-off* or a counterproposal provides more satisfaction than simply agreeing to a lower price. Giving away items or dollars will cost you money and weaken your credibility.

Why then do many of these well-meaning but ineffective negotiators drop prices or give discounts when no one asked for the concession? Perhaps they want to be liked. Perhaps they receive personal satisfaction from making people happy.

What if they found out that many people on the other side of the deal perceived them as lacking integrity? Customers will frequently walk away if they believe that there is no established price. Consumers, in this case, may just assume that prices are being made up on the spot. Worse yet, they may believe that some people are cheated while others get better deals.

Asking for some sort of *trade-off* for your discount is important, even if what you ask for isn't really worth very much. You can then respond to demands for concessions with yes instead of no. Agree to the other party's terms, but add your *trade-off* request as a modification. You can say, for example, "Yes, I can agree to that, if you will (*blank*)." This technique also allows you to keep the negotiating momentum on a positive note and moving forward.

Limit Your Concessions

Limit any concessions. Make several small concessions rather than a single large one. When you offer your Negotiating Nemesis a large concession early in the negotiation, you send the message that additional, larger concessions may follow. A major concession will seldom, if ever, endear you to the Negotiating Nemesis. It will only send the wrong message. You can be sure that your Nemesis will follow with another concession request. Reduce, rather than increase, the rate and size of concessions and set the stage for smaller, not larger concessions to follow. When discussing price, for example, if you begin at $100, then lower to $90, then $70, why shouldn't your Negotiating Nemesis expect $50 or $40 to follow? If your initial concession in this example were from $100 to $98, then your next reduction, if any, should logically be from $96 to $95. Do you see the difference this message sends? A word of caution is in order. There is a direct correlation between how much you familiarize yourself with this process and the extent of your ability to shift into it with relative ease.

If your early concessions are large, your Negotiating Nemesis may think that it's open season and ask for everything, including the proverbial kitchen sink. When that happens, it is next to impossible to return the negotiation to reality. If you argue your position, your Nemesis may assume that you have temporarily found your backbone and will undoubtedly wait until you cave in again. As a result, the deal gets postponed and could be lost forever.

Another reason to use the *trade-off* technique is purely an economic one. Logic tells us that the more you ask for, the more you receive. From now on it is important to view every negotiation with these simple principles in mind and apply them in combination.

Since most buyers and sellers focus almost entirely on price, they miss many opportunities to offer or receive valuable concessions such as financing, added features, faster delivery, or closing dates, and for additional or better services, including research and development. The value of these concessions to customers or clients frequently exceeds the initial cost of the basic product.

You Have Options

If you're the seller and the buyer asks you to drop your price, you still have options. You can *trade-off* rather than argue over price. You could say something like: "Okay, if you will double your order ... or , "If you'll sign an exclusive agreement that we alone. . . ." Or, perhaps you could respond with, "Okay, but we can't justify doing that within our normal production schedule. We will have to work your order in when we have slack time and have it to you in ninety days. . . . "

If the buyer asks for custom changes or customizing of specifications, you might consider replying, "Fine, but you will have to pay for the new plates and a change-over charge. . . ." or "Fine, but we only do that on large orders of. . . . "

If the buyer wants quicker service, then you can surcharge items, offer mixed lots, insist on an agreement that grants you the company's next order, or something else along those lines.

I've known several negotiators who used the *you-gotta-take-it-all* tactic. If these buyers had a *hot* market item and low supply (but not much ability to raise the price because of regulated prices or whatever), they packaged it with an item that was a dredge on the market.

For example, in selling properties from failed savings and loans, the Resolution Trust Corporation packaged one prime rental house with five good ones and one that they couldn't give away. It worked!

By simply changing the way you negotiate, you can

easily improve your success. Recognizing and practicing the critical but forgotten step of trading concessions is invaluable in helping you obtain more of what you want while maximizing the satisfaction level of your Negotiating Nemesis.

Begin practicing *trade-off* in everyday life with common purchases. You'll be surprised how easy it is, how well it is received and accepted, and how lucrative the results can be.

9
Negotiating with and without Attorneys

"Now that we have agreed on this deal, I'll just have my attorney review it, and I'll be ready to sign the papers."

How often have you heard that conditional acceptance? How often did the deal fall through? And, how often did it come back to you not even remotely resembling the transaction you and your Negotiating Nemesis worked out?

Large corporations usually have a distribution path that agreements must follow before a deal is signed. This procedure enables all concerned persons, including the legal staff, time to review the terms and conditions before the company commits. Small entrepreneurial operations and even some mid-size companies attempting to minimize overhead frequently use the opposite approach. They sign the deal and call an attorney if (and when) problems arise. Regardless of company policies, almost all decision makers encounter the *let my attorney look at it* demand from many would-be deal makers and customers.

Do you dare say no? Certainly not. To refuse customers legal counsel would, at the very least, make them suspicious. They could very well wonder, "What is in this contract that my opponent wants to hide? I'd better not sign this deal. Is this guy trying to pull the wool over my eyes?" The mental questions continue.

To refuse letting an attorney review a contract would most likely end the negotiation—and not in your favor. It would simply *end*. Moreover, if legal actions occurred later, you wouldn't want a poor, uninformed consumer telling the judge that you denied him or her the opportunity to show the agreement to an attorney.

How do you feel when you have an agreement with a person and that person wants to get the deal approved by an attorney? Everyone has experienced the horror stories of deal-killing attorneys who seemingly delight in nixing a contract or proposal. You have to wonder if that so-and-so lawyer will symbolically rip the bottle from the mouth of the baby? So, you cringe, say okay to the request for a legal review, and hold your breath. You view the process as a roll of the dice, knowing your number may not be showing after the attorney finishes with a sharp hand of hacking and thrashing.

There Is a Better Way

Never fear. Before an attorney disrupts your baby's food source, let's review a better strategy. To understand a person, system, or process, you must mentally shift your perception to the other side. In this case, that would be the attorney's side. Having sat on both sides of the bargaining table, as deal maker and as consultant to legal counsel, I am qualified to share the common concerns with you. Clients hire attorneys to protect them. Protection in the eyes of an attorney takes on new shades of meaning simply because it is the attorney's job to reduce exposure to a client's potential financial loss.

Even a lawyer will tell you, if you want zero risk, don't buy or sell anything. And, whatever you do, *never, ever* sign anything. Ridiculous? Of course. This approach would be like lowering the speed limit to five miles per hour in order to reduce the highway death toll. You could certainly walk away from any collision, but you wouldn't ever get anywhere either, except at a snail's pace. Likewise, your business will stagnate if you insist upon rejecting all risk.

Attorneys have some risk if they approve a deal, so to avoid risk, they will, at times but not often, *kill a deal*. No one can later complain of being advised poorly. We've all heard those pitiful stories from friends and associates: "I went into a deal, and my attorney should have kept me out of it." This whining automatically shifts the burden of failure to the attorney and away from the client. Clearly, attorneys have to protect you and themselves. A tough situation.

Give Attorneys Specific Instructions

When you give an attorney vague instructions such as "protect me," the attorney, in his or her role as your protector, may be strongly inclined to advise you to make major revisions to a proposed transaction or to suggest you decline the opportunity.

The attorney's position is understandable. In the first place, if your attorney says a contract is fine as written, you might wonder if you are being sufficiently protected. You'll leave the attorney's office thinking, "Why do I need him? Why is he charging me such an excessive fee for doing nothing? I wonder if he approves everything." In this scenario, you can clearly see the intangible incentive for the attorney who has received poorly defined or even indefinite instructions, to be motivated to find something (anything) to change in every agreement. Attorneys have to prove their value if they are to earn or at least justify their fees. In no way am I implying that attorneys are unethical or unfair. The very core of their job is protection—for you and for themselves. They are just doing their job. It is your job to give them better instructions.

Effectively Use Your Attorney

When preparing contracts for clients, I have, on more than one occasion, intentionally left a small problematic item in a contract just so the lawyer would have something to delete. This tactic works if you're careful. If the attorney finds something to redline, the attorney and the client feel more satisfied. The attorney did a thorough job. The client was protected. I (the Friendly Persuader) remained in control.

However, let me give you a word of caution. Be extremely careful with this tactic. Never leave in a point that is too one-sided. If your opponent's attorney has even the slightest inclination that you are a crook, or suspects you are, at best, a bit underhanded, the attorney will and probably should redline everything in sight. If you are caught at this, even if you're as honest as Abe, you will lose both your credibility and the deal.

You Are the Boss

You can and should use an attorney's counsel, but learn to reduce any negative effects by fully understanding an attorney's role. Attorneys, like accountants, financial planners, or other professionals, provide information and advice based primarily on what you tell them. As the principal owner or manager, you're the primary decision maker. Attorneys and other professional advisors are to be construed as an extended part of your staff.

People often fall into the trap of having an attorney, a doctor, or a CPA make decisions for them. If you pass complete responsibility for the decision making to the attorney, then that person becomes liable for thousands or even millions of dollars if the deal sours. By saying no to the transaction, the attorney loses nothing and appears to have earned the desired fee. You are protected. Nothing ventured, nothing gained, and nothing lost here. The attorney merely acts upon presented information. You ask for protection. You get protection — 100% protection — but you didn't get the deal that you obviously wanted or you wouldn't have been negotiating and calling your attorney in the first place. So, guess what? You lose again.

Remember that the attorney is an expert in the field of law, but you are the expert in your field. You know your business better than anyone. Under such conditions, it's no wonder attorneys kill deals. In a similar position, you would be inclined to do the same.

It is imperative to keep in mind that when attorneys choose the safe route, you could potentially lose the deal of a lifetime. It is your business and your proposed transaction. You are the team captain. You must take charge and lead the team.

Be Specific

Recognizing that professionals are in an advisory role, approach them with clearly defined instructions. Define for yourself and the attorney what you expect and need. You may be tempted simply to ask if there is a problem with the deal, but refrain from such comments. With vague questions and instructions, the attorney, always eager to minimize your risks and maximize the importance of fees, may advise you to either make major revisions, which would send you back to the negotiating table, or to just say no.

To avoid such incidents, be specific. Say to your attorney, "Please tell me all that I am obligated to do or pay under this agreement and what alternatives exist."

With these directions, you're allowing the attorney to provide the service you are paying for, that is, interpreting the fine points of the law. Conversely, you reserve the right and responsibility to make the business decisions. You should decide whether or not you are willing to pay or accept the price, offer the warranty, agree to delivery terms, and you bear the risks of the transaction.

Limit the Attorney's Role

With these guidelines, how do you handle the "run it by my attorney" request? The best way is simple. Take the initiative to define or, more accurately, limit the role of a client's counsel. As we've established, it is untenable to deny your Negotiating Nemesis legal counsel. Simply agree to the request, but limit the attorney's review to making sure the agreement is legal. It would be a good idea to have the reviewing attorney identify any provisions that are not legally enforceable and cite the statute or case that makes them unlawful. Although a provision in an agreement may be financially risky or imprudent, very few are illegal or unenforceable. If there are any, you will appreciate knowing them. By limiting the attorney's role, you have removed the yes or no power from the attorney, and you have shifted part of the attorney's power to your side.

The following phrases have worked quite well when I have used them while I'm sitting in front of my attorney.

Use them if they fit your situation:

> *I don't trust this guy. He has lots of legal knowledge and a sound background in this field, and I'm new to this field.*

> *I want you to go over this with a fine-tooth comb and look for any mistakes that I might be making. Look for subtle wording that might infer that I owe more money for XYZ than what is called for in the first part of the contract.*

> *I think this is a really good contract, but I'm unfamiliar with the UCC Code concerning this transaction. Paragraph number ten says that payment would be per UCC Code. Could you please give me specific instructions and details for payment to be made per UCC Code. Then, look over the rest of the contract and make sure I did not miss anything.*

> *If an alternative payment plan would be better, I would love to hear about it.*

> *I want to sign this deal. The other party's attorney prepared it, and the company seems to be straight shooters. If there is any way that I can safely sign it without changing a word, that's what I would prefer to do. Don't let me do anything foolish, but be as liberal as you possibly can be.*

Let me add another very valuable point. When it comes to negotiating with attorneys, quite often I simply refuse to negotiate directly with them. Why? Where the law is concerned, most attorneys consider themselves considerably more knowledgeable and they consider everyone in the public sector to be less knowledgeable. This means that if I negotiate directly with the other party's attorney, I will seldom, if ever, be given due respect. If I argue my position, the attorney, fulfilling the attorney-client role, will argue twice as hard. It is the attorney's job to protect a client, and the attorney, as I have said, will naturally assume that I know very little about the law.

It's just human nature. When we think we know more than the other side, we take a much firmer stand to defend our ideas. We feel we are in control and have a need to prove our superior stance. "We did go to school all those years, didn't we? We do have that degree hanging on our wall. Doesn't it give us the right to stand up for what we believe? We can't let this non-law person win the argument." See where this kind of thinking goes? Give it up. You can't win.

Do you have options? Always. To save time and frustration, I often hire my attorney to negotiate with an opponent's attorney. The extra expense of sitting and talking to my attorney and telling this professional what I'm trying to accomplish is money well spent.

During this meeting, I fully explain my ideas and strategy.

You see, attorneys generally have a tremendous attorney-to-attorney respect. On equal ground, they can negotiate on a level playing field. Both assume at the outset that they are equally adept in interpretation of the law. This level playing field prevents either attorney from completely butchering the other's contract. It's called professional courtesy, and we have all heard tons and tons of *lawyer jokes* dealing with what many believe to be, in this instance, an oxymoron. So, we won't get into any lawyer jokes here.

For example, the more agreeable attorney will kindly say, "I have a little problem with paragraph number eight." This gentlemanly way of introducing the area of disagreement will start a negotiation process that your attorney can more than likely control.

When letting your attorney talk for you, be sure that you clearly state your points of contention. Tell your attorney exactly what you will and will not forfeit. As important, make sure you have the *right* attorney representing you.

Negotiate for Yourself

Should you hire your attorney to negotiate your agreements for you? Generally speaking, I would suggest you avoid getting an attorney involved in the negotiation stage. However, the decision depends on the type of agreement. Most attorneys, particularly litigation attorneys, have ample practice in negotiations and have acquired higher negotiating skills. It is also true that some attorneys are just naturally better at negotiating than others. On the whole, though, many attorneys have little or no formal training in negotiation.

Consequently, if you're a sales executive or in a similar position where you frequently negotiate agreements, you often have enough expertise to negotiate agreements satisfactorily — especially if sufficiently trained in the art of negotiation. Besides, who knows the operations of your business better than you? To become familiar with your business structure, your attorney would prepare extensively and charge you for preparation plus other services. The entire process is cost prohibitive.

Some situations do, however, deserve the professional skills only an attorney can provide. Without hesitation, use an attorney when:

> *You're involved in a dispute that hinges on the interpretation of the fine print of a previously signed agreement.*

> *The other party has initiated litigation or litigation is imminent.*

> *The negotiation is over a personal issue such as divorce or the dissolution of a business.*

> *You're unable to talk with the other side without major disagreements.*

Don't confuse the dilemma of whether or not to use an attorney as a negotiator with the issue of obtaining proper legal advice. In many situations, you can better negotiate solutions yourself, but never fail to seek legal counsel for matters requiring a professional legal opinion. Although you can probably save money by skimping on professional services, it could be like trying to economize by removing your own appendix. The savings may be, at the very least, shortsighted, but the process will almost certainly be painful. Don't try to cut back where it doesn't make sense.

10
The Most Powerful Negotiating Weapon

The most powerful negotiating weapon is a double-edged sword, and one that all successful negotiators possess. If you do not have this weapon in your arsenal, you will find yourself woefully lacking in the negotiating world. As the television commercial implores, "Don't leave home without it."

This double-edged, must-have weapon is the skill of *asking questions* and then *listening to responses.*

There was once a minister who was brought into a new church to take over the flock. His first sermon was fantastic. It was a rousing talk entitled "Love Thy Neighbor."

The next Sunday even more people gathered, eagerly awaiting the opportunity to hear what the new minister was going to say. He gave the same sermon again. After the third Sunday of hearing the same sermon, the church leaders gathered for a meeting with the minister.

"Reverend, your sermon on "Love Thy Neighbor" is wonderful and one of the most inspiring we have heard, but when are we going to hear a different sermon?"

The minister squared his shoulders and answered, "I'll start talking about another subject just as soon as you folks show evidence that you have been listening to the first one."

Similarly, during negotiations, we often become so involved in the process that we hear but don't listen.

Learn to Listen

There are many factors to consider in developing listening skills. First, you have to *listen for opportunities*. This basically involves the process of getting as much information about the subject as possible. It doesn't mean letting the person talk as much as possible. Some people ramble. It does mean that you must stay fully and completely focused. While your Negotiating Nemesis is talking, you're supposed to be trying to discern and redirect deviations from the subject matter. When the other person starts in an area of particular interest to you, you can always increase the flow of the conversation in your desired direction.

If all else fails, you can always rely on that all-around best and simplest old-fashioned comment for drawing people out, "Tell me about it."

The second level of listening is *staying focused*. Too frequently, we're so busy thinking and planning ahead when someone else is talking that we become distracted and forget to listen to what is being said. This situation occurs because we have our own mental agenda. We're solving a problem in our head without listening actively or attentively. With practice, you can learn to listen more attentively.

Let Them Talk

I always carry a legal pad to negotiations. As my Negotiating Nemesis is talking and I periodically think of something I want to interject, I make a one-word note on the pad to remind me of the point, rather than interrupt the speaker. It's amazing how often that note to myself never gets interjected into the negotiation. By not interrupting the flow of conversation, I allow my Nemesis to continue talking on the subject until the person fully addresses my point without my having to mention it.

Imagine how disruptive an interruption might have been if I had acted otherwise. You cannot learn anything while you're talking. You only learn when someone else is talking. When your Negotiating Nemesis is talking, you should encourage that talk by being an attentive listener.   Ask appropriate questions, if necessary, to spur more conversation, and then listen, listen, listen.

Listen for What Isn't Said

The third level of listening involves listening for what is *not being said*. The higher your degree of expertise and experience in negotiating, the more these techniques become obvious. Generally speaking, you should not expect your Negotiating Nemesis to come directly to the point. You seldom, if ever, have a Nemesis enter the room and declare, "I'm here to make a deal. Let's get it done and go home."

Usually, the person will talk around one subject or another, making one point to draw attention to another. A Friendly Persuader learns to concentrate on detecting such instances through the flow of the conversation and mentally analyzes what the Nemesis is dancing around. The Friendly Persuader will then concentrate on those conclusions.

Let me give you an example. If the Negotiating Nemesis is talking about the financing of accounts receivable, you can bet the farm that there is a cash-flow problem. The underlying assumption may be that the Negotiating Nemesis could be faced with laying off employees or that problems exist on the assembly line or in distribution or problems with shipping. As you intently listen to this person's comments on accounts receivable, you may properly deduce that the real problem concerns disgruntled or unhappy customers who fail to receive their orders in a timely fashion.

Solve Their Problems

Very few people make major commitments to solving a problem until they get in touch with the *emotional cost* that the problem creates. In other words, someone may tell you about a problem but avoid telling you the depth to which that problem bothers or affects personal decisions. You may have to probe to uncover this raw nerve, but exploration at this point is well worth your time. If you experience this syndrome surfacing during a negotiation, you can anticipate the discovery of the Achilles heel of your Negotiating Nemesis.

Once your Nemesis stops talking, analyze what was said and what was not said. See if you can come up with questions that will stimulate the bringing of more information to the surface. Usual questions include: "How do you feel about that?" Or, you might also ask, "How does that affect your company, and how does your company see you in relation to this issue?"

Stay Sharp, Act Smart, and Concentrate

Success in this critical area depends upon the level and intensity of your concentration. Stay sharp, act smart, and concentrate. A Friendly Persuader should always remain aware of an old Irish saying my Grandma often used, "The Lord gave us two ends – one to sit on and the other to think with. Success depends on which one we use the most."

Proper use of the listening tool can catapult your negotiating skills. Using it can transform mediocre results into unqualified successes. Since few people listen intently or effectively, it's unlikely your Negotiating Nemesis will recognize the tactic or use it against you. Listening is less than a natural skill for most people, but with effort and practice, you can learn to listen effectively.

Listening intently to the other person can:

> *Reveal the true interest of the speaker.*

> *Provide the alternatives you need to make an offer that will close the deal.*

> *Provide feedback on what you have offered thus far.*

> *Indicate what other concessions you can ask to receive.*

> *Let you know what the competition is doing.*

➤ *Reinforce your personal relationship with your Negotiating Nemesis.*

➤ *Let you confirm that your Negotiating Nemesis has a proper understanding of your side or position.*

➤ *Make your Negotiating Nemesis feel good about the deal.*

➤ *Let you control the negotiation.*

➤ *Build credibility.*

You will get all this, and more, just from asking questions and listening to answers. However, you must do both. Asking questions is not enough. Stop and listen to the answers. What is your Negotiating Nemesis saying, and how is he or she saying it? *How* a person conveys information is almost as important as *what* a person says. Tone, mannerisms, and facial expressions transmit a wealth of information.

For this reason, I personally find e-mail unsatisfactory for some business transactions. Now, I know that e-mail is the wave of the future and many of you are prepared to defend it as the only way to go. And, while I use e-mail as much as the next guy and completely agree that it has been one of the most important communication advances of all time, I acknowledge that e-mail does tend to dehumanize the art of communication. E-mail messages are short, simple notes that use abbreviations and often are scanned quickly. E-mail allows for no back and forth dialogue, and these dialogues enable us to clarify points that others may misunderstand. A phone conversation is often a better solution, and a face-to-face meeting is preferable for important discussions.   In a face-to-face meeting, you are able to readily spot misunderstandings and correct them instantly. You can also visually see how the person is responding, allowing you to pinpoint subtle shifts in tone, mannerisms, and facial expressions. The difference between a successful and an unsuccessful negotiation could very well hinge upon this one point.

It is also important to mentally prepare yourself for negotiations. Any negotiation worthy of your time is worth mental and physical preparation. When you ask questions, simply remind yourself to *be quiet and listen*. These four words can be vital to your position. Learn to remain silent rather than shooting back a reply.   In most instances, people would rather you listen to them than agree with them.

Use Your Weapon to Your Advantage

Since we have established the skill of listening as our most powerful negotiating tool, it becomes a valuable weapon in our negotiation arsenal. We must then focus on how we can effectively use this weapon to our best advantage. First, weapons require ammunition for power. We all know that knowledge is power. Having power on your side can make the difference in whether or not you get what you want.

To gain knowledge, you must have a way to gather it. Listening to your opponent talk is the easiest way to gather valuable information. How else can you collect so much information from your Negotiating Nemesis? There is no easier way to get this data. It could take weeks, months, or even years of research or investigation to uncover the facts that you will be able to grasp in just a few minutes of listening. And, these are facts that you need. So, not only does listening provide important ammunition that you need to fire your weapon effectively, but the information flows quickly and is practically cost-free.

Load the Weapon

Now that we have the weapon (listening) and the ammunition (knowledge), it's time in our negotiation process to *load the weapon*. To execute this procedure properly, we need information. A Friendly Persuader needs to know as much about the business alternatives of the other side as is humanly possible. Never assume your Nemesis will choose or value the same benefits you choose or value.

Specifically, you should identify the underlying reasons your Negotiating Nemesis wants to make a deal, not just what is said during a conversation. What is said is vital to your negotiation strategy, but you must also uncover any underlying wants and needs.

People you negotiate with will seldom begin their side of negotiations by revealing the issues they consider critical. They may have, and more than likely do have, some personal drives or desires involved besides business or financial interests. Take a moment to explore the possibility.

Your Nemesis may:

> ➢ *Seek recognition*

> ➢ *Seek understanding*

> *Seek career advancement from the transaction*

> *Perhaps a person merely needs someone to listen to HIS or HER problems or interests.*

A word of caution. At this point and time you really mustn't concern yourself unduly with the merits of the personal wants and desires of your Nemesis. For you to involve yourself in this area too deeply would be counterproductive to your focus. It is only important that you *know* that such feelings or attitudes are present with your Nemesis and then *seek* them out so you can effectively deal with them. Then, get on with the negotiation. Remember, we're here to drain the swamp.

Load Your Weapon "Properly"

Loaded with knowledge of your Negotiating Nemesis' business, financial, and personal wants and needs, you're now properly prepared to negotiate. You can suggest mutually beneficial solutions and be equipped to offer the right benefits. Depending upon your storehouse of knowledge, you may even be able to, as the expression goes, "Sell them oranges when they want apples." Don't count on it, but it does happen. Yet, it only happens when you have fully and properly loaded weapons.

Ready, Aim, Fire

On the side of my computer monitor, I have taped a quotation clipped from a financial magazine. My perceived value of this quote is evidenced by the fact that it is the *only* thing taped to my monitor. It is a constant reminder to me that my goal should always be to reach a conclusion. The quote is attributed to T. Boone Pickins of Dallas, well known entrepreneur and chairman of Mesa Petroleum: "Be willing to make decisions. Don't fall victim to what I call the 'ready-aim-aim-aim syndrome.' You must be willing to fire."

Having the most powerful weapon on the battlefield, fully loaded with proper ammunition, is of no value unless you use it. Prepare yourself for battle. Fire the weapon — begin the negotiation. Once the weapon is fired, the first, second, and third rules are all the same — *Listen*.

Keep quiet long enough for your Negotiating Nemesis to talk. Ask open-ended questions that your Nemesis cannot answer with yes or no. You may ask about new products or services, plans, expansions, current problems, or current events that influence the industry's decisions.

When an answer surfaces, encourage that person to expand on the answer. Ask, "How is that going to work?" or "What else are you exploring or planning?" The harmless encouragement, "Tell me more," also nudges additional thoughts to be shared with you. Once started, most people like to talk about their businesses, their jobs, and especially themselves. After all, we think about ourselves most of the time.

You may be surprised how much a person reveals if you have the patience to listen and to appear interested. Keeping the conversation focused on your Nemesis should be easy. When needing to describe the benefits of doing business with you or your company, do so in terms of what your Negotiating Nemesis receives, not what you receive. For example, don't bluntly say, "This contract with you is the largest one our company has owned." Instead, you might comment that your company assigned this account to you because it is your job to work with only the biggest and best clients. Furthermore, you'll guarantee the lowest unit cost your company can provide.

This technique, called a *reframe,* allows you to redirect the focus on the client's or customer's benefit. By stating that the client's account is the largest your company has ever received, you emphasize your client's power. You tell too much. By rephrasing your words, you shift the focus from the *client's power* to the *client's worth.* You boost your client's ego by saying, "The company and I have decided to treat you as a VIP, and your account will get the best." This second statement is the same train of thought with an entirely different spin.

Besides talking about business issues, you have two other procedures to follow in using the *listening weapon.* First, always try to fill the other side's personal and business needs. Continually listen for revelations of personal needs expressed by your Negotiating Nemesis.

These may include:

> ➤ *Recognition – My boss will really notice me if this deal closes.*

> ➤ *Security – My job will certainly be protected if I get the best price.*

> ➤ *Esteem – The other people in my department will appreciate what I obtained for them.*

It is imperative that you readily assume that your

Negotiating Nemesis favors a particular communication style. One person may want cold facts while another seeks to feel, from the very beginning, that the best possible deal is being made. Another may need to fully explore the inner workings of the deal.

If possible, use the form of communication your Negotiating Nemesis prefers. If the person requests to see how the deal works, then you should show charts, graphs, pictures, and other visual evidence of benefits he or she stands to gain. By listening early in the negotiation process to discover your Negotiating Nemesis' preferred form of communication, you'll soon start speaking the same language.

Hitting the Target Twice

It's possible to hit the target twice with one shot if you use the listening weapon properly. Not only will you know what to offer and how to present the offer, but you will also gain a bonus. When you attentively listen, your Negotiating Nemesis will be flattered and will view you as a person who is genuine. This allows for the personal relationship building process to continue its forward movement while keeping the flow of communication in play.

Good Eye Contact

Another form of communication is good eye contact. This technique, learned in speech class, shows your interest in the person or persons with whom you are communicating, and it generates a response from audiences indicating that they are aware of your interest in them. For some people, especially men, direct eye contact is somewhat uncomfortable. Here's a tip. Try focusing on the other party's nose, just between the eyes. The person will never know you are looking anywhere other than the eyes.

Keep the Communication Going

A good way to let your Negotiating Nemesis know that you are listening is occasionally to ask, "Let me see if I understand you correctly," and then repeat your version of what was just spoken. Confirming in this way assures your client or customer you are both listening and that you understand desired wants and needs. Such assurance builds trust and boosts your credibility while increasing the chances of the relationship prospering.

Don't Let Your Weapon Backfire

In firing your negotiating weapon, be careful of backfires. Just as the listening weapon can ensure victory, it can bring defeat. Neither before nor during a negotiation should you reveal information that can damage your negotiating stance. For example, avoid saying that you "have to close this deal in two weeks or lose $1.5 million in guarantees" or that you have to "finish by 5 p.m. to catch a plane" or any similar confidential or potentially weakening information. Even something as seemingly harmless as, "Do you think we can wind this up by 5 p.m.?" can backfire on you.

I have heard that this ploy was used on us in reverse by the North Vietnamese during the Paris peace talks. When the American delegation established its presence in Paris in anticipation of the beginning of the talks, our space and accommodations were arranged on a week-by-week basis. It quickly became known that the North Vietnamese government had its delegation sign five-year leases. Is it possible that we gave evidence to the negotiation process that we wanted out of the war, and we wanted out as soon as possible?

My Worst Negotiation Defeat

Carefully formulating plans, doing your homework, and lining up avenues for making a negotiation flow smoothly, are important, yet you can and should expect, at times, to encounter problems. Prepare for the unexpected, for it will undoubtedly happen. Negotiating disasters do occur. Not even the best Friendly Persuader can fully control what team members will say or do.

To help detour this problem, brief your technical and support people and caution them against speaking too freely. Silence, as we have demonstrated, is a powerful negotiator. Breaking silence can cost you and your company far more than you may at first realize. I know first hand. Once when a partner spoke too soon, I faced my worst negotiation defeat.

As chief executive of a real estate development firm, I had been leading the effort to develop a master plan, with a joint-venture partner, on a parcel of land we owned in a major resort area. For almost a year, we carefully explored development options, conducted studies and surveys, determined the best use for the property, and compiled a list of prospective joint-venture partners for finance, development, and management.

At the top of our list was a potential partner who could fill our needs on all three levels. The prospective partner was financially strong, a national leader in the industry which we had determined to be the best use for our property, and had an internal management team already active in the field. To top it off, this potential partner was a closely held private firm (meaning it should have been easy to get to the right person and obtain a quick decision) and, believe it or not, was based in our geographical area — almost in our backyard.

This deal was almost too good to be true. All we needed was to *get to the man*. Ours was a home-run project . . . perfect for us and perfect for the partner. All that remained now was to inform our targeted company that it was going to be our partner. As it turned out, it was not quite as simple as that.

To prepare for the negotiation, we researched the company and its internal power structure. Within a week, I had confirmed the name, position, and power of my soon-to-be Negotiating Nemesis. We'll call him Andy. Now, Andy was executive vice president of the firm and a member of the board of directors. He was married to the daughter of the founder of the firm and was the father of two school-age daughters. In his mid- to-late forties, Andy was a few years younger than I.

One of the first things I looked for was the answer to the most logical question, "Is Andy for real, or is he *just* a son-in-law." To my delight and excitement (the adrenaline was really flowing, and I had not even met him yet), we learned that not only was Andy *real,* he was *really real.* A top graduate, with honors, from a top school, Andy came from a good family with a strong business legacy. He joined the firm soon after college and his marriage to *the daughter.* Shortly after joining the firm, and quietly behind his back, Andy was being credited by his peers with having given the company a *kick in the butt.* Expansion, revenues, and profits had soared under Andy's guidance. Superman, right?

What really got me going was that, almost universally, our study revealed that Andy had quickly earned the reputation of being one of the "best negotiators in the country." Now, I'm really going— totally fired up. I can't wait. All we need is a proper way to get to Andy, so we can start at the top.

A member of the board of directors of my company had a contact. It was a friend-of-a-friend type thing that usually doesn't work, but here it did. It seemed that Andy's company had been considering our very area as a prospect for some time and was actively looking for just the right parcel of land. Andy, reportedly, was excited to learn that we not only had a choice location for a project, but that we had also done much of the background development work.

Our director came back to me with the burning inquiry, "Andy wants to know how soon we can meet with him." I had died and gone to land-development heaven.

We quickly organized a meeting. Of course, Andy had invited us to his office. Home turf, you know. The meeting was to consist of Andy, his associate (the acquaintance of my director), my director (so he and the associate could exchange pleasantries), the president of our firm, and me. My team met early, before the meeting, in a coffee shop just across from Andy's corporate headquarters, so that I could give my two associates a last-minute summary and review of what I intended to do and how I intended to do it. I had a perfect plan. After all, it had been in development for months. Although I hadn't met him yet, I knew my Nemesis better than I knew anyone else in the world — that is except for Elvis, the Pope, and the President of the United States.

I was ready to start. This debate would be a classic case study in the art of negotiation. I could almost feel history in the making as I concluded my summation to my associates with a final flourish. I revealed my closing strategy. Perfect checkmate. I was prepared to lead Andy through the negotiations until I had him hooked (committed). I was convinced that Andy needed this deal as much as we did. I was certain he would accept all terms.   If asked to do so, I would have staked my career on my belief that the only real point of contention, the only point Andy could find to negotiate, was the price of the land.

As we mentioned earlier, a negotiator who can only talk price, loses. Did you get that? Loses. No matter what else Andy said, he simply had to like everything else about our proposal. And, I had him on the land price issue.

I carefully explained to my associates how I planned to set Andy up. After the initial exchange of pleasantries, I would begin talking about the project. At this point, it was important that they both sit quietly — as in "Don't say a word." In fact, I specifically informed them that as I ended a certain dissertation involving the price, I intended to *absolutely stop talking*. I further added that after a particular phrase, I would not speak another word until Andy spoke. I didn't care if it took an hour or a week. Andy had no option. He wanted the deal, and the only way he could get the deal was to acknowledge our price.

Okay! My associates understood — no talking. Everything went exactly as I had planned and predicted. I was on a roll. You know the feeling. You are speaking or making a presentation, and you can just feel that you're doing a great job. That was *Yours Truly* on that fateful day.

I then came to the critical point of checkmate. I finished my last epic line, stopped talking just as I had told my associates I would do, leaned back in my chair, and kept my eyes focused on Andy.

Silence. Andy had to speak. When he did, victory was ours. I knew it. Andy knew it. Minutes passed like hours. The silence could be heard in China. I could see my victory in Andy's eyes. He was trapped into replying.

No one moved. I didn't even breathe. The deal was mine any second now... not minutes... not tens of seconds ... but seconds. One... two... (he's mine)... three... (I wonder if Andy has ever been defeated before)... four... (I may go down in history)... five... and then my world came crashing down.

My director said (and the words still ring in my ears), "Now, Andy, we really want to do this project with you. If you can't make it work with this price structure, I'm sure we can work on these numbers a little more."

I could have killed him. I may yet. Of course, we lost the battle that day. Weeks later, we did manage to salvage some semblance of the original deal, but rest assured that it was not in our best interest. Andy kept his streak intact. Why? Because of an associate's momentary slip of the tongue. He still doesn't know why he spoke out. He certainly had no intention of doing it. The words just slipped out. Like so many people, my partner could not stand the pressure of silence!

Clearly, as it happened here, it can happen to you. You could bow to the pressure, and you can never caution your staff, associates, and administrative people enough. The weapon shoots where you point it. Don't let it backfire on you.

Listening is the most powerful negotiating weapon you can own, and now you know how to use it effectively. While your competition attempts to hammer home ideas of what your customer or supplier wants, you can glide through the deal, calmly and confidently, and close it.

Listen and win.

11
Playing the Trading Game

As a knowledgeable negotiator wanting to increase an order and save money, you might well ask, "If I increase the size of my order, how much will you reduce the cost per unit?" Such questions are often encountered. When you give something, you expect to get something in return.

Avoid Being Demanding

Asking for (and receiving) *trade-offs* is part of the negotiation process as we have learned. Another vital ingredient is understanding, practicing, and becoming proficient in trading concessions. The key here is in *asking*, not *demanding*. When you demand anything, whether it's a discount, more service, or better value, even if you deserve it or have an absolute right to it, you must always anticipate facing *resistance*. It's just the nature of the beast. Humans like to be asked, not told.

As a Friendly Persuader, you are anxious to keep more of what you have, and you seek to get for yourself some of what your Nemesis owns. Paradoxically, your

Negotiating Nemesis is out to do the same. This situation sets up an interesting challenge, a reason to negotiate. The stronger the demand, the greater the resistance, regardless of what either side forfeits. Most people spend most of their time concentrating on what they can do to benefit themselves, so if you want to get their attention, you have to speak a language they understand.

Ask Virg

Just ask Virg, my former father-in-law. Virg and his wife, Til, traveled extensively throughout the world, mostly for pleasure. They had a proclivity toward conducting day-long souvenir hunts, and Virg considered himself particularly proficient at overseas shopping.

As the traditional head-of-the-household male, Virg was in charge of negotiating all souvenir purchases. His approach was based on the belief that despite which country he was in, the native language, and the educational level of the shopkeeper, he could communicate if he spoke slowly enough and loudly enough. His reverberating shouts of "HOW...MUCH ... IS ... THIS?" have been widely reported around the world.

Obviously, this is not what we are talking about when we say you must speak a language that your Negotiating Nemesis understands. Instead, we think of language as a meeting of the minds. In other words, translate your request for more of anything into terms of how your request benefits the other party. It might appeal to the person's greed factor, it might assure the person that he or she will not lose the deal, or it could be any one of the vast number of other motives we have encountered. Whatever it is, you must speak the other person's language. Make sure your Negotiating Nemesis understands clearly and decisively exactly what you are talking about. Don't take anything for granted. Translate everything into *how it benefits your Negotiating Nemesis.*

For example, instead of asking for credit or extended payment terms because your company needs the money, mention that the additional credit will allow you to increase your order. Or, you could comment that a lower price would allow you to bid on another job, which would require another order sooner than expected.

You Ask — They Counter

Trade-offs naturally follow *Asking for it.* You ask. They counter. Conflicts in the *trade-off* stage largely depend on how good a job you do of asking. Let's review some key factors.

Whenever you ask for an item, you must have a reason for asking and be prepared to state your request in terms of benefits for your Nemesis — the person or company involved in the negotiation. Otherwise, your Negotiating Nemesis may ignore your request. Most of us already hear too much about what somebody else wants from us every day. Nevertheless, our ears perk up when someone has something to give us.

Why? Because it happens so seldom. If you want to gain your Negotiating Nemesis' attention, turn the discussion to what you can offer or give in the transaction. When you do, I can assure you that the person across from you will listen attentively. You speak the opponent's language when you describe benefits.

Sometimes you face difficult or economically unfeasible demands from the other side. Your Negotiating Nemesis may demand a 25% price reduction due to new competition. Let's assume that the new competitive threat is real. Let's further assume that you simply cannot handle a 25% reduction. Rather than categorically refusing the request determine more precisely the real needs of your Negotiating Nemesis.

Find out why there is a need to cut price. Maybe there's another way you can address your opponent's needs. If during dialogue, you discover that bookkeeping is a problematic area with your Negotiating Nemesis, perhaps you could modify your system to fit that need. If you can keep your Nemesis from entering invoicing information twice or perhaps can provide electronic invoices on a disc or by e-mail, you can win the person to your side. In this case, you use your efforts to reduce the client's internal costs as a *trade-off* for the price reduction.

Companies frequently modify product specifications, such as leaving off frill features that aren't necessary for some customers. Redesigning services or features could, therefore, afford you another possible counter proposal to a price reduction.

Let's assume that in the previous situation the 25% competition is real. However, you know that your product has certain features that, while not essential to your Negotiating Nemesis, certainly tend to make your product more attractive. Maybe they will not be 25% more attractive, but they will perhaps be favored to some degree between 0% and 25%. Point out these advantages or features, along with the long standing business relationship that your two companies have enjoyed, and mention that you expect to be a reliable and valuable supplier for years to come. In the process, you are subtly saying you're not sure how long the new competitor will be around.

Be careful. Don't alienate or put your Nemesis on the defensive. As negotiations proceed, try to combine your advantages into a package. Wrap it up with a bow consisting of a discount rate you can afford. If you've completed your homework and truly know your customer as you should, it's likely that you can salvage this customer. Salvage enough customers, and you may send the new competitor packing.

An effective Friendly Persuader explores all options before succumbing to the final line of failed negotiation: "I cannot match the lower price."

12
The Power of Red or Green

You will see better results from your negotiations if you always offer the other side a choice: "Do you want the red or the green widget?" Borrowed from the retail sales business, this approach forces your Negotiating Nemesis to make a choice between two alternatives, both favorable to you, rather than seek out a yes or no decision which leaves you with a 50/50 chance of winning (or losing).

As a potential buyer, a favorite approach of mine is to offer a low cash price or a higher price with installment terms or an agreement with several contingencies. Usually, I have little concern for which option the seller selects. Since I have carefully thought them through in advance, I know I will win regardless of which choice the seller makes. While busy mulling over decisions, the seller is generally too occupied to realize that, in either case, I will have my needs met.

This multiple-choice offering is particularly effective in real estate purchases. It greatly enhances your chance of getting what you want on your terms. Just be careful not to offer a smorgasbord of choices.

Too many choices lead to confusion. Limit the alternatives to two or three. In fact, two seems to usually work best for me.

Several benefits occur when you give people choices. Obviously, when people make choices, they feel as if they are in control. The more your Negotiating Nemesis feels this power, the better. You want your Nemesis to *feel* in control—not particularly *be* in control.

This concept is similar to many magic tricks I've read about in "How To" books. I've always had an interest in magic but never took the time to become really good at performing tricks.

In one trick, for example, the magician sorts and shuffles a deck of cards and then lays them out in three rows, "A," "B," and "C" and in three columns. The magician asks someone from the audience (for a hypothetical example, let's say that person is you) to pick a row. The magician knows the hidden card is in row C. You pick row A. The magician says, "Okay, you decided not to use row A, so we'll put it away. Now, you'll get to pick another row." If you pick B, the magician says, "Okay, that's the other row which we won't use." The magician then starts working with row C, which was the row he desired in the first place.

If you had picked "C" as your second choice, the magician would have said, "Okay, we'll work with this row that you've chosen and put away the other ones."

You're probably thinking that this trick is so obvious. Not so. I've seen dozens of tricks performed like this over and over again with such flare, smooth hand movement, and confident use of voice that no one thought twice about it. Likewise, when you give people choices, you're letting them choose, but you've pre-determined which choice is going to benefit you.

If you walk into a car dealership and the salesperson asks if you prefer the caramel red or midnight blue, you can rest assured that there's no car in stock in any other color. You will only be given choices that the salesperson knows will lead you toward buying a car today. You need to put together your choices in the same way. Not only will you have the benefit of making the other person feel in control, but you will also move that person further down the path you already know is the path that best suits your desires.

The second great reason for providing choices is that they help you see how your Negotiating Nemesis is thinking. With each choice the person makes, you get more insight into how the person makes decisions and also an indication of the trend of personal preferences. The more you know about your Nemesis' preferences and decision-making patterns, the better off you will be when it comes to asking for what you want and offering *trade-offs.*

The third reason for incorporating choices in negotiations is often overlooked. If you give people choices and the deal falls apart, you can always go back and start over at another time.

In a great television program where I was interviewed about investments and money matters, the hosts repeatedly asked the question, "What do you do when you've reached an impasse?" I thought this was strange behavior for such experienced hosts of such a prominent show. I later found out that they were trying to renegotiate their contract with the network and had reached an impasse!

My response was simple, "If you're at an impasse, go back and look at all the choices you've made throughout the negotiating process. If you review choices and see room for some potential changes that can be made, you can probably reopen the negotiations at that point. This technique allows you to lead the direction of the negotiation down another path more favorable to you rather than down the dead end that you have already discovered."

Choices Are Powerful

Choices are a powerful and often overlooked negotiating tactic, especially when dealing with customer service situations. Customers prefer choices. When you come up with a solution for the customer, add an alternative solution. This *additional* or *secondary* solution will be one you know the customer will never choose. You may, for example, tell a customer to buy another product and return the "defective" one to the manufacturer. Always be sure to try to offer two reasonable choices, only one of which you expect the customer to choose. The slightly less reasonable one is just so the person can have a choice. By offering them choices, you make your customers feel that they are in control.

While in college, I sold mutual funds. My firm represented more than 130 mutual funds. I originally thought it inappropriate for me to make choices for potential clients, so I prepared careful background comparisons for about sixty different mutual funds and custom molded them into a presentation that I had carefully personalized for my client.

I soon learned that people can't choose from sixty possibilities. After receiving my beautiful presentation of sixty options, almost every client came up with analysis paralysis. Being a brilliant, young college student (I was young and a legend in my own mind), I promptly came up with a solution. I decided to condense my sixty selections. Through careful study, I came up with *one* terrific you-gotta-have-it fund. Who better than I should decide, from the original 130 mutual funds, the one that was absolutely perfect and, therefore, acceptable to my prospective clients? After all, I was a college man.

Surely my sales would now soar. I would storm in proudly announcing that I, from all the mutual fund offerings in the world, had selected this mutual fund especially for them. Since I had done my homework, I knew this particular fund, an aggressive one, was the perfect selection for someone exactly like this client. Confident that I was ready to snatch victory from the jaws of defeat, I went on with my spiel.

Guess what? I promptly lost 75% of my prospects because 75% of the people did not want an aggressive fund. I've never forgotten this lesson because this experience taught me much about offering choices in negotiations.

> *You must give choices.*

> *Make sure the choices you offer are selections between product one and product two or at least between products one, two, or three.*

> *Never offer more than three choices. Too many choices can be confusing.*

> *Two choices are best. Most people prefer to make an "a" or "b" selection – this one or that one, red or green.*

Timing Is Important

Timing is not only important, but timing is everything. What you gave the other party last year, last week, or even the last time you met, is history. Don't expect to get any consideration for what you gave up in the past. Similarly, never make a concession thinking that doing so will be appreciated in the future. The first rule is never give away anything without receiving some reciprocal contribution from the other side. However, the reverse is not necessarily true. Just because you have received a price break, better terms, or other benefits or consideration doesn't mean you automatically have to give up anything. If the other side doesn't ask, don't offer.

When you must make a concession, start small and get one in return. Concessions don't have to be equal, but they have to have *perceived* value in the eyes of the receiver. Training, product support, sharing research and development data, warranties, or excellent service are frequently more valuable to the buyer, yet these worthy offerings are often taken for granted by the seller. Because different companies have different cost accounting centers, an account executive who offers additional service or support may not have to place a dollar value on it.

Good Stuff and Junk

Whether you're selling or buying, attribute the appropriate value for all you offer in the transaction, especially for self-styled price buyers (those who say they want to compare price). Always offer to give up what the other side values and you don't value. Next, ask for more of what you do value. Think for a moment what the results of this could be. You wind up with all the *good stuff* and your Negotiating Nemesis has all the *junk*.

The trading of concessions is an important part of satisfying needs in negotiations. Don't give your best offer and then use a take-it-or-leave-it approach. You may think your offer is more than fair, and it might well be, but it won't necessarily appear that way to the other side. Negotiation involves building and maintaining a relationship as well as exchanging concessions. Of particular importance in the *trade-off* phase is the need to keep personalities separate from the subject of the negotiation. You frequently see attorneys illustrate this key principle. They argue over a point, zealously advancing their respective clients' interest, and after the debate go off to have a friendly lunch together.

It is vitally important to always remember that people like people who are like themselves. The more you mirror your Negotiating Nemesis, the more comfortable that person will be with you. Nothing really *happens* in a negotiation until the parties are comfortable with each other. Then, and only then, can you begin to build a relationship. If you don't have a core relationship with your Nemesis, you might as well fold the table and go home.

Saving Face

Finally, you must be careful to build a path that is open for your Negotiating Nemesis. Even if you receive a great deal from a negotiation, in the end you must leave your Nemesis with an opportunity to look good and/or have a great story to tell. This is especially important if there is even a remote possibility that you will conduct business with that person again. In most instances, your clients or customers won't care quite as much that you got all the good clothes as long as you don't send them home stark naked.

In taking care of the relationship, it is also important not to attribute the other side's offers or rejections to the person. Instead, attribute them to that person's *cause*. Don't be offended when your customer tells you the competition offered a lower price or implies you're making excessive profits.

No matter how heated a negotiation session may become, preserve the communication channel so you may continue to negotiate effectively. Interject humor, if possible, to keep all exchanges friendly, and, if necessary, consider substituting negotiators so the process continues in a positive vein if and when a personal relationship deteriorates.

By presenting requests in terms of benefits for the other side, offering alternatives, assigning values to your concessions, and keeping the personal relationship between negotiators strong, you will win the trading game.

13
N.L.P. and D.I.S.C. as Negotiating Tools

Now, let's get a little technical. Just when you thought it would be safe to sit back, relax and compliment Ol' Barney on giving you a nice "easy" read, it is time for us to consider the fact that there is some psychological basis in even what seems to be the most casual approach to negotiating.

Since negotiations are really about relationships, much insight can be gained from the field of psychology.   Looking at theories and techniques of why and how people behave and relate with one another plays an important role in conducting effective negotiations.

One set of tools, which appeared in the 1970s and still applies today, is Neurolinguistic Programming, commonly called NLP.   Two noted psychologists from San Diego, Drs. Bandler and Grenlin, are credited with originating and developing the hypothesis of NLP. The basic premise is that certain human behaviors are tied with experiences that we tend to repeat and reinforce until the behavior and the emotion are closely tied together.   One way of making behavioral change is to interrupt these normal behavioral patterns and establish different patterns to use as guideposts for new behaviors, thus establishing a new norm.

We Are Conditioned to Say No

In sales training, for instance, we teach salespeople that they have to ask a potential buyer to buy the product or service at least seven times, on average, in order to close the sale. Why is this true? One reason is that potential buyers have been conditioned to immediately say no when someone asks them for their money.

Parents start this trend when young children accompany them to the grocery store.   The wise grocer positions the tasty candy at an adult's knee level, which is exactly at fingertip height for a small toddler. The first time a child grabs the candy, the child hears no from the parent. The second reach for the candy, even if the child asks permission first, usually sparks a second no. Repeatedly the child reaches and by now is begging for the candy. Three or four no reponses generally change the worn-down parent's to a yes. Some children have learned that Mom and Dad are good for nineteen no responses. Since most children are somewhat pushy with parents, if the yes answer hasn't surfaced, many will press for the twentieth attempt.   Parents, on the other hand, are simply trying to teach delayed gratification (and a little bit of nutrition).

Despite the best efforts of the parents, the child has learned that repeated asking or begging will bring the desired answer. They also learn that no does not necessarily mean no. It means no for now and yes in a little while. This pattern, imprinted subconsciously in the child's response pattern, is not only difficult even as an adult to break but is often unnoticed as a behavioral pattern. Psychologists tell us that as adults we behave in set ways because of societal and environmental programming. This programming affects our negotiation abilities in our business and daily interactions with those around us. When aware of such behavioral patterning, if a change is desired, it is up to us to *consciously* change it.

Later in life, when we first learn how to get a good bargain at a garage sale, we're told not to seem too interested. In these and many other ways, we're trained to say no several times until we absolutely convince ourselves there is either value in the purchase or we simply cannot live without it.

Saying Yes Takes Time

Of course, as adults, there may be many reasons other than behavioral patterning, for a no response. A no response from us might be a test of our opponent's negotiation abilities or techniques, or we may simply be inspecting that person's honesty. We may also want to become more comfortable with the idea of owning the item before we admit even to ourselves that we will purchase it. For many, it takes time to get used to the idea of parting with money. Our natural inclination, and for most a behavioral pattern set in childhood, is to keep our money in our hand as long as possible.

Based on these principles, it is easy to see why those raised during the depression years tend to hold onto money longer than those growing up in the baby boomer years. While some hand over money easily, for most, parting with money consumes mental and emotional energy and, therefore, takes time because we have to adjust our thinking.

Sales People Know What No Means

The savvy salesperson is very aware that the first no is a conditioned response. If the customer says no and then walks away, the customer probably means no. If, however, the customer says, "I'm just looking today," and then hangs around the counter, there is still a very good chance a sale is imminently possible. Savvy salespeople know that each objection or question concerning the product or service represents another chance to move the prospect closer to a yes answer, which means a sale.

Effective salespeople realize, too, that while buyers generally base purchasing decisions on logic, emotions also play an important role. This clerk or dealer will ask a specific question or a series of questions that will enable a customer to internally feel the excitement, joy, and anticipation of ownership.

These questions, geared to analyze the ways that a potential buyer customarily receives praise and gratification, are also effective avenues for gaining valuable customer information. Does the customer like to hear things? Does the customer like to see things? Is the customer the touchy, feely type? Just how do you motivate this person? Answers to this type of query enable the clerk or dealer to push toward a sale.

All of these techniques relate to Neurolinguistic Programming, the idea that we are programmed to respond in particular ways. Like the informed salesperson, the better the Friendly Persuader can determine the Negotiating Nemesis' conditioned response, the better the Friendly Persuader will be at successfully communicating on an appealing and winning level.

Building a Comfort Zone

A primary principle of NLP is mirroring and matching. If you learn to skillfully copy certain characteristics or behaviors of the person with whom you negotiate, that person will feel more comfortable working with you. This doesn't mean that you mimic your Nemesis in so obvious a manner that the other person clearly recognizes your attempts. Stage or fake responses are seldom, if ever, effective. You simply aim to emulate your Nemesis so the person will be more comfortable discussing business with you.

In fact, I don't really believe in changing who I am. I believe my strongest selling point is *Barney being Barney*, and your strongest selling point is you being you. Some days I wear jeans and on other days three-piece suits. My dress code depends upon the cliental I will meet throughout the day, the type of meeting, and the importance of the meeting.

The dress for success idea is certainly effective but as important is the idea of mirroring your Nemesis. If the person you are doing business with is more comfortable in jeans and you show up in a $800 suit, the person may feel uncomfortable discussing business with you. It all depends on the situation, the type of business transaction, and the type of personality you are facing in that particular instance. You must first know your Nemesis or at least know what you think the person expects and then try to mirror that image.

Mirroring is useful because it helps me build a comfort zone for my Nemesis, and the more comfortable that person is with me the more trust that person will have in me. So, within the range of what *is* me, I take time to *adapt* me, to *dress* me, to *poise* me, to position me in such a way that I am as much like my Nemesis as I comfortably can be.

I recall dozens of situations where I've used this technique. One example stands out in my mind. As is always the case, I could control only part of the situation. Others aspects simply fell into place. Since this was a business meeting with a major executive whom I had never met, I dressed according to acceptable dress codes for such a meeting. When I walked into the room to meet him (with my size, well let's just say that from frame to floor there is a lot of me present when I walk into a room), this man looked like my bookend. We both could have played "pulling guard" for the Dallas Cowboys.

As we sat chatting, we naturally had a built-in camaraderie: "You know, you gotta fly first class" and such as that "because you don't fit in coach." During the conversation, he told me he obtained his undergraduate degree at the University of Missouri, and I silently prayed he received his master's degree at Northwestern as I had. With so many common interests, I knew, without a doubt, we were heading toward a close. This concept will seldom, if ever, fail. The more you build rapport, the better you can negotiate with your Nemesis.

In order to establish a harmonious relationship, I always consciously search for common ground and build my conversation around this potential bridge. I consider my years as a Boy Scout to be an important part of my life. If given an opening, I guarantee you that I will mention Boy Scouts at least once in any conversation. If I find that my Nemesis was a Boy Scout or a Boy Scout Leader or has a son or nephew who was or is a Boy Scout, I will talk about Boy Scouts.

Of course, many techniques and procedures help build rapport, but asking questions during polite conversation is perhaps the quickest and easiest way to exhume points of commonality.

D.I.S.C.

The second psychological discipline that has an impact on effective negotiating is the D.I.S.C. System of Human Behavior.

The *D* relates to your *Drive Quotient;* how much of a driver are you? How much of a driver is the person you're negotiating with? Does your opponent want to get things done and get them done now? Is your Negotiating Nemesis accustomed to being in charge or will he or she languish at the low end of the productivity scale? Is your Nemesis laid back, compliant, or even complacent?

The *I* relates to your quotient for *Influencing* others. If you have a high *I,* you are probably a talker and a socializer who feels the need to be around other people. A low *I,* on the other hand, applies to those people, and we all know them, from whom you seemingly have to drag information. With them, even a casual conversation is, at best, difficult and sometimes next to impossible. These people spend little time talking about themselves and preferably avoid talking about any other topic if at all possible.

The *S* relates to the *Swiftness* or *Speed* of your

movement. Are you a frantic-paced person who enjoys working on ten projects at once? Perhaps you, in contrast, are a *pipe smoker*, the exact opposite of *swiftness.* A pipe smoker, often referred to as a *chess player*, represents the type of person who sits back and contemplates each move before making it.

C relates to *Consistency*, or your desire to follow the rules. Where are you on that scale? Be honest now. Ol' Barney grades on the curve and does not tolerate cheating, even by his most loyal followers. Consistency in action is an admirable trait for any Friendly Persuader. Without it, you not only knock your Negotiating Nemesis off guard, but you will frequently trip yourself up, too.

Why is this D.I.S.C. information important to us in the study of negotiations? If your usual behavioral responses are exactly like those of your Negotiating Nemesis, you're going to have a much easier time reaching agreements. You will understand each other. You'll communicate in the same way and at the same level.

If, however, your Nemesis is opposite to you in any area or worse yet *in all four areas*, then you have a tough decision to make. You can either ignore what I'm discussing (which, of course, I don't recommend) and experience an absolutely uphill grind in communicating information or reaching an agreement, or you can modify your style before it's too late.

For analysis purposes, let's assume that you are a high *I*, which means you enjoy talking. Silence in conversations irritates you. Not only are you the life of the party, but sometimes you are the only life that keeps the party alive. Your Negotiating Nemesis is, however, a low *I*, a pipe smoker. Your Nemesis not only pauses between sentences, but it seems that the person also pauses between pauses. This pausing grinds your nerves.

When facing this dilemma, if you know the concepts of mirroring and matching and D.I.S.C., you could either use them or choose to ignore them and proceed on your merry way. Of course, with the latter, you would fill every silence with an interjection. On top of that, you'd probably end up spilling your guts and spilling the beans. You would talk and talk until your Negotiating Nemesis knows everything necessary in order to obtain an absolutely super deal from you.

Conversely, if you are familiar with these techniques, and you wisely choose to use them, you will immediately repress your actions. You will slow your speech pattern, which will, in turn, make your Negotiating Nemesis more comfortable.

If your Nemesis has previously pegged you as an excessive talker and expects to readily gather information from you, then your change will throw the person off guard. Since pipe smokers absolutely believe that people who talk fast are, at best, trying to outmaneuver them and, at worst, trying to cheat them, your mirroring technique will serve you well.

Despite your Nemesis' previously conceived notions of you, your new image will build his or her trust and confidence in you to your advantage. Furthermore, when you slow down your speech and actions, you will hear important information rather than merely hearing the sound of your own voice.

This slower, more focused YOU will help to avoid rambling. With more time to analyze your Nemesis, you will, likewise, make more powerful arguments and will use far fewer words. This confident and focused

YOU will enable you to bond quickly with a *pipe smoker* because pipe smokers are genuinely uncomfortable with people who ramble.

Being aware of these concepts and techniques and utilizing them wisely will enable you to quickly and easily turn a potentially disastrous negotiation into a much more manageable event—even, perhaps, an unqualified success.

Personally, the tougher the situation, the more likely I am to throw out an anchor and ask myself, "What is my immediate purpose in this negotiation?" or "What tools do I need to be relying upon to make sure I fulfill my purpose?" These discerning questions often save the negotiation day.

Let me tell you about one of the earliest times that I remembered all these principles and actually put them into practice. I call it Daniel and the Lions' Den. Notice that I'm confessing how difficult it is to keep these tools and philosophies uppermost in your mind. To implement them effectively in the heat of a negotiation is difficult if you are not fully cognizant of your own subconscious actions and the actions of others. Mirroring and matching more than once has helped me save an otherwise lost deal.

Daniel and the Lions' Den

I once signed a contract to purchase an apartment complex and had placed $25,000 earnest money as a deposit. I knew of several investors who would be highly interested in partially or fully financing this particular transaction for me, so upfront money was of no concern. However, a major interruption occurred shortly after all parties signed the contract. The broker (the agent for the seller) called and said another potential buyer had presented him with a backup offer to purchase the property. This new backup buyer's offer was $50,000 more than I had contracted to pay for the apartment complex.

Now, it was unethical and probably illegal for the broker to bring a third party into the negotiation. The broker made it fairly clear that this transaction was open for me to *flip* the apartment building to his new buyer. Forgive me, folks, but when it comes to money, particularly in the range of $50,000 in quick profit, I am weak. I probably hesitated a full two or three seconds before I said *yes*.

To further complicate matters, I was then living in another state from where the apartments were located. Keeping in contact with and on top of a long-distance transaction is much more difficult than a local deal.

When time came to close on my contract, the broker said there were problems. Surprise! Surprise! He said there would be a delay because the buyers who were offering the fifty grand weren't quite ready yet ... but, yes, they still wanted to buy the apartment building. I kept waiting for this unscrupulous broker to add *trust me* at the end of his remarks. To his credit, he didn't.

To make this portion of a very long story short, I discovered one day, just before the scheduled *double closing,* that the new buyers were not going to buy the apartment building at all. They had put up only $5,000 in earnest money as a deposit, and they were willing to walk away from it.

What a dilemma! Here, I had $25,000 at risk and was going to have to tell the original seller why I wasn't able to close on my contract. Naturally, since I was depending on the permanent financing from the new, suddenly invisible buyers, I had not bothered to put my financing in place. Somehow, incredibly, the broker felt no guilt in this matter, but I soon changed that for him.

Naturally, I dreaded the meeting with the owners of the apartments. I was totally embarrassed, and I had every reason to believe that they would keep my $25,000 earnest money deposit and find another buyer. Legally they could. When the owners learned the truth about my desire to *flip* the building to a new buyer for more money, they could readily conclude that they had priced the property too cheaply. To make matters worse, I knew that one of the sellers (the female) had a blowtorch temper and that it would be on white-hot.

When I walked into the room, I felt like Daniel entering the lions' den. There were three unfriendly faces on one side of the table. The female owner of the property was there along with her husband who generally said little and who had recently undergone triple bypass surgery, which might have come from holding in his emotions. The third face was the broker from hell. The property owners had a reputation for always being in charge, and they knew how to effectively manage money. I knew this deal hurt them in more ways than one.

The broker, sitting back and seemingly indifferent, fully expected to receive half my deposit toward his commission on the proposed sale, plus one-half of the $5,000 deposit which was being forfeited by his *flip* buyer. He seemed to have no idea that his representing me as a seller before I bought the project from his clients was a conflict of interest that could make him subject to losing his real estate license.

With my second step in the door, I slid into the nearest seat. The last thing I wanted was for me (at my size) to be towering over everyone and exuding the impression of power. I felt it important to exert as little power and control as possible. I felt that it was important for everyone to feel as comfortable as the situation would allow.

I leaned forward, elbows on my knees, head bowed, and looked up at the female representative of the property ownership. I did not need to look at anyone else; she was in charge.

"I'll bet you're really upset," I said.

As expected, she launched into me. She had liked and trusted me. She felt I was someone she would like to see own the property. She had offered owner financing to me...to me...not some stranger. Her tirade seemed to last forever. I waited until she seemed to have exhausted all her arguments. I then asked if there was anything else. I asked her husband if he had anything to add. No one else spoke.

"I can see why you feel that way," I slowly began. "I would have felt that way, too, if I were in your shoes and had only seen your side of things. I know this all looks bad, but there is another side to the issue here."

"Yes, it is true. I had originally planned to buy the apartment building along with my investor group and was looking forward to a long-term investment. This real estate broker (I said this like I was referring to the Devil himself) called me with an offer of a quick $50,000 profit if I would flip your apartment building to another client of his. Like a fool, I fell into the trap and relied on others."

Silence filled the room as I reached for my Franklin Planner. In the front, I keep pictures of my kids. I held the picture so the husband and wife owners could get a clear view. "Do you remember from our first meeting how we both talked so much about our kids? You have three sons, grown kids, to be proud of. I have three small sons . . . sons that I want to send to college just like you sent yours. I saw that $50,000 as enough to get them all into college. I didn't talk to you about it because this all seemed too quick and too simple . . . too good to be true . . . and posed no harm and no threat to anyone. I also, like you, trusted the word of this agent," I continued, throwing only the slightest glance toward the agent. "But it seemed that what he promised wasn't for real. You might also be thinking that the apartments are perhaps worth more than I agreed to pay you. I thought that at first, too, but they must not be worth more since the deal I had for more money fell through, right? My offer, I felt at the time and still feel, was top dollar for the property. So, it appears to me that the deal we had between us was at the right price all along."

Since I clearly had their attention, I continued. "But I do know one thing for sure. This forfeited $5,000 earnest money deposit that the broker has is not really mine. Unless you extend my contract, I can't buy your apartments." Having concluded my performance, I reached for the $2500 check that the broker had made out for me. Remember now, the deposit was for $5000, and the broker was going to keep half. I turned it over, endorsed it, and handed it to her. "This money really should be yours—no matter what you decide to do."

Unbelievably, tears welled up in her eyes. She turned to her husband and said, "See, I told you he was a man of character." Turning back toward me she asked, "How much more time do you need?"

I asked for six months. The broker practically fell out of his chair. He knew control had shifted from his side of the table to mine and that he was facing the eventuality of putting the $25,000 back into his escrow account for a very long time. No paycheck for him, at least not for some time. He asked to speak to the sellers in private.

The sellers extended my contract for two months. That was enough time for me to complete the deal. This is not just a real estate story. It is a classic example that shows how using mirroring and matching techniques can help you communicate more closely and more in-depth with people and perhaps mend an otherwise broken relationship that would undoubtedly put an end to a deal. It is about being very much aware of the state of mind of your Negotiating Nemesis and dealing with that first, well ahead of speaking personal thoughts. It's an excellent example of successful negotiating under pressure.

A Friendly Persuader will surely add the tools of N.L.P. and D.I.S.C. to his or her negotiating toolbox and learn to use them effectively.

14
Perceived Power Is Real Power

Let's explore your feelings when you negotiate with a prospective employer or with a loan officer at your bank. Doesn't it seem that the employer or loan officer is in control of your fate? In fact, didn't you actually begin feeling out of control at the very moment the appointment was first scheduled? Of course you did, maybe even to the point of dreading the meeting, although it was vitally in your best interest. On the appointed day, you probably missed breakfast, cut yourself shaving or smeared your makeup, and had a tough time selecting your wardrobe.

This feeling is only present when you believe your Nemesis has power over you. It is true that in any negotiation, having more power than your Negotiating Nemesis can enable you to receive more of what you desire from the transaction. No wonder you feel ill at ease over the bank meeting. You need the bank more than it needs you.

While the bank may or may not need your business, you need the loan to buy a home for your family, fund a medical emergency, or to expand or save your business. Naturally, you are nervous over the meeting. On the other hand, your Negotiating Nemesis (let's call him Tom), the bank officer, had a good night's rest, relaxed while eating a filling breakfast, enjoyed an unscathed shave, donned a suit that looked like it was tailored just for him, and paraded toward the bank with a bounce in his step.

Why the difference? Tom is in the power position. He may or may not make you a loan. It's his decision. No matter what he decides to do, when you leave the bank, he'll simply get another cup of coffee and move to the next file, whereas, your financial future could be on the line.

Similarly in a job situation the prospective employer may hire you, may hire someone else, or may decide not to hire anyone. The employer holds the decision making power and will make the decision based upon what is in the company's best financial interest. You have no power. Or, do you?

In the bank or job situation, it might appear that your Negotiating Nemesis has all the power, but perception and reality may not be the same. To gain power, you must believe you have power even if it looks as if you have none. If your negotiating stance for a job or loan were as weak as it appears, then there is nothing to negotiate. It would more nearly resemble panhandling.

We've all been in situations where we felt powerless and possibly assumed it was fear of the unknown. But, now we know better. It's not fear of the unknown that rattles us. Our fear stems from our own subconscious. Although we are less than fully aware of our actions, our conclusion that we have no power and our belief that our Negotiating Nemesis has it all literally turn the

table that way. In such a situation, we concede power
to the other side without knowing it—and certainly
without putting up a battle.

What Is Power?

Power is often granted or conferred to either us or
our Nemesis. Yet, you are still wondering what you
should do if you fear you have little power. Surely, Ol'
Barney doesn't want you to think your way out of this
incident. Then again, perhaps he does.

You must first realize that power is always relative
to the situation. If you have control or authority over
a person or a situation, you have power. If you can
influence another person's decisions, you have power.
Other than in the military (and it's not even conclusive
there), power does not come solely from title, rank,
position, or name.

Does a corporate vice president have power over a
production worker? Possibly, but if that worker is the
only person who can complete a special task for the vice
president, and both the executive and worker recognize
it, isn't that worker in a position of control? Any person
in control of any situation, whether office manager or
clerk, holds a certain amount of power.

Unions are a good examples of powerful groups
that, when they decide to strike, can drastically change
the power structure of a company. When workers
strike, they halt production. Each day workers strike,
the company suffers financially. Managers or
administrators must then negotiate to settle the dispute.
Without workers, a plant loses money and will most
surely close.

Clearly, the notion of power correlates to the

situation. Just because a person controls one situation, the person may or may not control another.

Always remember that being in control may be easier than you think. Control simply means that you have more power than your Nemesis. Without knowing it, you may actually have that power and just do not realize it.

Since you often don't know how much power you have in a negotiation, it is just as easy to believe you have power as it is to believe that you have none. Sometimes there is just no way to know. But, always remember that a person who feels powerful, acts powerful. I know you've heard it before, but it really does work that way. We've all heard of the *Think Yourself Rich* concept. But, have you ever tried it?

Unlike some disciplines, power in negotiations can be as much illusion or appearance as it is reality. Let's call this concept *perceived power,* and *perceived power* is the only kind that counts in a negotiation. Even if your company has the best services or products at the best price, if you're naive enough to assume your customer is aware of these facts, you risk negotiating with little power when, in actuality, you had a great deal of power available to you.

Conferred Power and Perceived Power

Obviously, parents have power over their kids. Right? I am the proud father of teenagers. By all rights, I'm in charge. I'm in charge partially because I make up the rules for my household, and, equally as important, I'm still twice their size, and size does carry power. But, size alone doesn't give me any real power. I have no power unless the kids give it to me.

Reality is different from perception. To begin with, I lose power and control if I fail to earn and maintain my kids' respect. When I earn my teenagers' respect, they confer a certain level of power to me. This conferred power is what we call perceived power.

Reality is less important here and perception takes front row. If, for example, you're currently negotiating for a contract that must be signed to prevent your company from folding, and if you're the only one with this information, you can negotiate with the same power as the finest blue-chip competitor. The power you have is the power your Nemesis perceives you to have and not your real power. Actually, you have none in this negotiation, but no one knows that except you. When in a tight position, never let your Negotiating Nemesis see you sweat.

Staying in control or allowing others to believe you are in control is the first step toward increasing your negotiating power. Since your power depends on your Negotiating Nemesis' perspective, you would be wise to find out what that person's perception is of you. If you are intimidated in a job interview because you're worried that the employer has the power to reject you, your fear may make you so nervous that you perform poorly. Your fear, not your lack of ability, kept you from being hired. Fear and frustration are negative energies that transfer from one person to another, and on the whole, people are intimated by their own and other's fear.

If we turned any one of these situations around, we would have a different picture. How do you know the bank officer isn't on probationary status by the bank for not processing and approving enough loans? Isn't it true that banks have to lend money to stay in business?

Or, perhaps the job interviewer was desperate and needed to hire someone quickly. Now, if you had possessed this knowledge before the meeting with the banker or the interviewer, wouldn't your perception have greatly increased your sense of power over these situations. Knowing these facts would make you more comfortable negotiating, wouldn't they?

I once discovered perceived power when borrowing money for a large scale land development. I had already borrowed beyond my set limit, but with land developments, additional funds are generally needed. I desperately needed extra money, so I called and made an appointment with the loan officer, Mark Goodson. After spending several days rehearsing my talk, a speech so well crafted that I knew it would induce my Negotiating Nemesis to lend me more money, I confidently approached the bank.

Upon arrival, I started the conversation with Mark with a little light humor by saying, "You know, Mark, I've figured out how to help your bank make more money."

"How's that?" Mark asked.

"I need another loan, and the interest rate I'm willing to pay will add a great deal of profit to your bottom line."

Much to my surprise Mark asked, "How did you know that at the loan committee meeting this morning we were told that we hadn't been making enough loans this month?"

Rather than letting the cat out of the bag, I just smiled and said, "Intuition."

The truth of the matter is I had no idea what had gone on that morning. I knew Mark had been on vacation, and I knew that he generated most of the new loans for the bank, but I had no way of knowing that a decrease in new loan volume had been the main topic of discussion at the loan meeting that morning. Because of the earlier meeting with his associates, Mark saw me as an asset and not as a borrower. Naturally, I received the loan.

Pump Up Power

With this concept in mind, you can clearly negotiate from a position of power on every deal. Certainly, many situations may be less than favorable, but always look for ways to boost your perceived power. Begin by attempting to find out whether the employer, loan officer, customer, or whomever you are negotiating with, is under pressure to make a deal. Asking the innocuous question, "How is business?" can trigger a person's dialogue. To move the conversation to more specific information, tactfully quiz with a more detailed question such as , "Have you had many orders for your Gizmo NXQ-77?"

Expect a positive response. Carefully listen as information emerges. Perhaps business is strong. Don't let that discourage you. A strong or healthy business doesn't mean that the game is over. Initially, the person could be withholding information. Your job is to pump up your perceived power. Even if you think business is strong, and that your services are not needed, keep your face muscles and body movement relaxed. Your outward appearance makes you either a strong negotiator or a weak prey.

Since deciding the power status of your Nemesis can be difficult, especially if your Nemesis is trained in the art of negotiation, the next step is similar to holding all the valuable cards in a high stakes poker game. If your card hand is strong, you feel inward confidence and can, without saying a word, exercise your control and power to those around you. Everyone in the game knows who is in charge of the next hand. With confidence and pride, imagine that your Negotiating Nemesis really needs you. Don't get cocky, even if you think you have more power. Just remain confident. You will be amazed at how well your Negotiating Nemesis will follow your lead and assume you have more power if you act as if you are empowered.

The reverse is also true. Your Nemesis will react conversely if he or she senses that you lack confidence. Confidence is contagious. Fear is contagious.

Remember the law of the jungle. If you display confidence, those who would devour you will give you a wide berth. But, if you appear weak or afraid, you could get eaten alive. This is just as true in corporate America as it is in the deepest regions of the jungle.

Don't Exaggerate

In attempting to dramatically escalate your perceived power, you may be tempted to fabricate, exaggerate, or misrepresent facts. Don't. It could be a fatal mistake, either now or at a later date when it comes back to haunt you.

It is important that you never, ever promise more than you can deliver. Any false statement or misrepresentation about you, your company, product, service, or property can be deadly. When your Nemesis finds out the truth, and the person surely will now or later, your credibility and power will be destroyed. Lost credibility is seldom, if ever, fully replaced. Guard yourself against making this fatal mistake. It will cost you in the end.

Sleepless Nights

A good illustration of negotiating power is the old story about the man who couldn't sleep one night. He tossed and turned in his bed, turning the light off and on. He was obviously in nocturnal distress. At 3:30 in the morning, his wife raised up on one elbow and yelled, "What's the matter with you? You've been driving me nuts tossing and turning, and I'm not getting any sleep."

Her husband replied that he had borrowed a large sum of money at the bank, and it was due tomorrow. He then explained that he was not only unable to pay the money that was due, but he didn't even have the money for the interest. The banker was a friend who helped coach their son's soccer team, and the man didn't know how to face his friend.

The wife reached across her burly husband, picked up the phone, and started dialing.

"Who are you calling at this hour of the morning?" he asked.

"I'm calling Ted, our banker."

"Don't do that. You'll wake him up," the husband said. "What could you possibly have to say to him?"

"Hi, Ted," she said in a cheerful voice. "This is Marjorie, Bill Martin's wife. I thought you ought to know that we can't pay the loan that comes due tomorrow. In fact, we can't even pay the interest. Sorry to bother you at this time of night. Thanks and good night." As she replaced the phone, rolled over, and prepared to go back to sleep, she added a comment to her husband, "Now, let him worry about it. It's his problem."

Assessing who really owns a problem is frequently

difficult. We often take our own pessimistic viewpoint and assume that the problem belongs only to us. With a faulty loan payment, the real problem rests with the banker, the person who lent money to a risky client. The worried man, as a borrower, had more power than he perceived. He simply had to find a way to pay his debt on *his* time and not on the bank's time. Here, the banker, if he considered the man to be honest, would more than likely extend the loan or try to work out a suitable plan. The man had more power than he thought, and his wife proved it to him.

In any negotiation, whether with a banker, employer, client, or whatever the case, perceived power will maximize your chances of negotiating more successfully.

218   THE NEGOTIATING PARADOX

15
Fighting Back

If you feel alone and unarmed on the negotiation battlefield, it may be because you fail to recognize the artillery being used against you. Spotting the techniques used by others will allow you to better defend yourself. When you know how to counteract these ploys, you are back at the control panel. You are in charge. Let's look at a few popular negotiation tactics you may face in your quest to become a Friendly Persuader and see what you can do to defuse them.

The *good guy/bad guy* presentation is one of the oldest tricks around, and it is, surprisingly, still effective. Here's how it works. A team, typically of two, meets with you. Even though they begin negotiating as a unified team, at some point one person stubbornly disagrees with your every request while the other is supportive and understanding of your position. As negotiations progress, you clearly view the supportive person as your ally and the other as your enemy. Whether you are aware of it or not, you have just encountered the *good guy/bad guy* routine.

When it appears the *bad guy* is almost ready to walk

out of the negotiation, demanding ever more, the *good guy* approaches you. Having gained your confidence by appearing to be on your side, the person may say, "If you can give in on just this one item, I think I can talk my irrational partner into continuing with the negotiation."

The team may either repeat this process or use some variation of it. Each time they approach you with a new proposal or point, you agree in an attempt to salvage the deal. You believe this is a reasonable reaction on your part. After all, the *good guy* has been supporting you and your position, and maybe he has forced the associate to listen to your side of an issue. Meanwhile, you make concession after concession as a favor to the *good guy* in order to keep the *bad guy* from walking away from the deal.

Only after the team has duped you out of many benefits do you realize the opposing team planned and carefully orchestrated the entire charade. This scenario appears often in police interrogations on TV shows. Real law enforcement agencies still use it effectively. What is so surprising about the *good guy/bad guy* routine is that although everyone has heard of it, seen it, or even tried it, the gambit still works.

Defending Yourself

What can you do to defend yourself from the *good guy/bad guy* ploy? First, you must recognize the tactic. When you find yourself mysteriously befriended by an opposing negotiator, be suspicious. Your blossoming friendship may be based on ulterior motives.

Now, here's the antidote. With humor ask, "You aren't going to pull that *good guy/bad guy* routine, are you?" Or, you might inform the *good guy* that you will attribute everything the *bad guy* says to both of them. If you call this technique to the other side's attention, the opposing members will probably stop playing the game.

Lowball

Another tactic is the *lowball offer*. If you've ever shopped in a car dealer showroom, you've probably experienced this tactic. It works like this. The seller gives you an unexpectedly low price in the early stages of your discussion, usually just as you're leaving to view the inventory at another dealer. By offering such a low price, the dealer attempts to discourage you from shopping around. If you do seek additional price quotations, other sellers most likely won't match the lower offer. It appears as if you were lucky and will save money on your purchase.

Unfortunately, when it comes time to close the deal, the seller forgot to mention a few important items such as extra charges for normally included items. For example, transportation, delivery, or dealer preparation, which you thought or *assumed* were included, are now extra. Or, you are told that the sales manager has to approve the deal, and when asked, the manager naturally refuses the terms. The dealer then imposes other terms that make the deal less attractive. By now you have wasted half of your afternoon and have little time to shop around.

To protect yourself against a lowball offer, specify all terms and conditions of the deal. Make no assumptions. Get every detail in writing. To be enforceable, all deals in excess of $500 must be in writing. Always remember that if a deal looks too good to be true, *it probably is* too good to be true. An old rule of thumb is that those who shop price alone must be prepared for a rude awakening. A low price often ends up costing more.

Red Herring

A more sophisticated technique, sometimes seen in political negotiations, is the *red herring* tactic, the practice of focusing on one point while intending to sneak a more critical provision into the deal. While politicians point the spotlight on each other's wrongdoing, voters must search in the dark for each politician's real stand on controversial issues. That's why the line item veto was so important to the U.S. President.

Before the adoption of the line item veto, members of Congress would find a bill that the President loved and tie a send-money-to-my- friends-and-the-people-back-home provision to the amendment with full knowledge that the President would have to veto the entire bill to defeat the *pork barrel* amendment.

Similarly customers may probe about quality or price, posing as reluctant buyers, when actually their company desperately needs extended credit terms from the sale. Just because the focus of the negotiation is on a particular issue, it may not be the most critical one that has to be resolved.

The *red herring* technique is difficult to spot, but if you do see it, shifting the discussion to the other side's true concerns will neutralize it. If your Negotiating Nemesis obviously spends a disproportionate amount of time on issues that are clear, trivial, or have already been resolved, you can rest assured that something is amiss. Look for a hidden agenda. Once you identify those concerns, you can better evaluate the deal and probably will negotiate additional, valuable concessions from your Negotiating Nemesis. Effectively and thoroughly preparing for the negotiation will also help you discard *red herring* techniques.

Phantom Bidder

We call another potentially more treacherous negotiating tactic *the phantom bidder*, a ploy based on the notion that competition spurs lower prices and better terms. Companies or individuals seek lower prices by telling their Negotiating Nemesis or leading them to believe that there is competition when, in fact, there isn't. The goal is to deceive the seller into lowering prices or offering better terms. It is slightly amusing, and certainly profitable, when suppliers use *the phantom bidder* ploy and customers fall for it. New account reps, investors, or inexperienced negotiators are particularly susceptible to this seemingly harmless technique. Eager to win the contract, the unsuspecting negotiator responds quickly to better the offer from the competing buyer.

Few can avoid matching or beating a competing bid simply because they erroneously feel it the only way to bring closure or make a sale. Negotiators who use this technique are betting that you won't indelicately ask who the competing bidder is or that you will not find out that the phantom bidding competitor simply does not exist.

Defending yourself against the unknown is more

difficult than identifying competition and developing a successful strategy to win. The danger is that there may actually be another buyer. The key to effectively combating *phantom bidders* is to know the marketplace, including your competition. If you must face this formidable foe, you have a right to know who it is. Go ahead. Ask the question: "Who is it?"

Large corporations, institutions, and government agencies may have bidding procedures that preclude identifying the competition. If such is the case, you simply have to do your homework. It is comforting to note, though, that most of these organizations won't employ *the phantom bidder* technique as a matter of principle.

As with all strategies, there is always more than one line of defense you can use against the phanton bidder technique. If you know your opponents well enough, and you should, you can probably tell whether they are being truthful. This is yet another good reason for being familiar with your customers and their business. If you cannot find out who the other supplier (or buyer or seller) is and believe a real one does exist, ask questions: "What did they offer that I didn't?" or "How can I stay in the race?"

The more you understand how you are uniquely qualified to deliver needed services, the better you will be at showing your Negotiating Nemesis that despite money, your proposal is still the most favorable deal. Reliability, warranty, and similar quality items are always valuable benefits you can point out as a counter to an unseen opponent who beats you only on price. This is true whether you are facing a phantom bidder or some other foe or obstacle. By understanding these concepts, you will be in a stronger negotiation stance.

You-Must-Do-Better-Than-That

Finally, there's the *you-must-do-better-than-that* negotiating tactic. When someone responds to an offer with this phrase, watch out. The demand seems natural, but don't buckle under pressure. Inexperienced negotiators will blindly follow the other side's request for lower prices or better terms. Unilateral concessions can harm your negotiation power and credibility. The Negotiating Nemesis may then ask, "Why was the price so high in the first place?" Or, the person may continue to ask for concessions until you finally say no.

Respond to the *do-better* request by asking, "Why?" followed by, "How much better?" If you're really expected to *do better*, it's up to you to define how much better and why. Otherwise, there may be no limit to what others may ask you to forfeit. The danger is that some negotiators routinely make this request. It's almost a no-lose proposition for them. Stop them and make them defend their request. At this point, offer a concession for their demand.

Recognizing and defending yourself from these negotiating weapons will build your negotiation armor. If you are aware of these tactics, you can use them when appropriate to turn an attack around.

16
I Can't Afford It

The "I can't afford it" response from a customer or client has little to do with the person's financial resources, and as a Friendly Persuader, you must be aware that the difference between customers or clients buying goods or services and their ability to purchase those items are often on opposite ends of the spectrum. A person who wants and/or needs your product or service will find a way to afford it.

It's a shame that many salespeople and even executives spend their careers trying to sell potential customers products and services that the customers don't want or need. Yet, everyday, many spend valuable time touting the merits of their wares to prospects whose basic goal seems to be to refrain from buying. Prospects respond to the hard-sell barrage of figures, specifications, pricing structures, and delivery arguments, simply and negatively. They dismiss the confusion with four little words: "I can't afford it."

More often than not this phrase really means, "I'm not interested." How can you avoid wasting your time with customers who give this response? Maybe you could talk only to cash-rich prospects. Maybe you could just, automatically and without being asked, lower your prices. Guess what? Neither of these approaches will produce significant results except to make you or your company poorer. Fortunately, there are several ways to defuse the "I can't afford it" response. With this response removed, you will spare yourself and the customer the frutration and discomfort of such a ploy while increasing your chances of closing a transaction or producing a sale.

If They Want Apples, They Won't Buy Oranges

To become a Friendly Persuader equipped to overcome the "I can't afford it" roadblock, you must propel yourself over two traditional hurdles. First, a person who wants and needs apples and does not need oranges won't buy oranges, even at a discount. You can successfully transcend this first barrier with relative ease if you take time to screen your potential client. It is highly inefficient to spend valuable time meeting and negotiating with people who don't need, can't use, or aren't ready for your products or services. For example, it is more than likely useless to try to convince a fledgling manufacturing company with twelve employees that it should computerize with a multimillion dollar mainframe when the firm now operates successfully with a couple of personal computers.

A big discount will not change your or your customer's circumstances. Of course, it is important to keep in contact and maintain a business relationship with any company as it expands. As companies grow and mature, they admittedly remain true to and do business with those suppliers who contacted them early and remained in touch as they grew and prospered. Always screen customers and clients. Know what they want. Then, try to fulfill that need.

Know Your Customer's Business

Screening enables you to familiarize yourself with the workings of your potential customer's business. This evaluation process is crucial to the first negotiating step, *planning and evaluating*. At this stage, you must take time to learn all you can. Quality suppliers know the industry, the competition, and they know exactly how their product or service will meet the present and future needs of their customers. Many business operators immerse themselves so completely in the day-to-day operations of their business that they fail to spend time sorting out trends. Remember that if you fail to know your Nemesis' wants or needs, you aren't negotiating. You are simply shooting in the dark and wasting your time and resources. Preparation for negotiation prevents you from pushing apples to orange buyers.

The Inevitable Happens

Overcoming the second hurdle requires knowing that there's no such thing as a person or company who "can't afford it." What this response really means is you haven't proven that your product or service meets your Nemesis' needs. When a Nemesis believes either that there is a need for an item or that he or she simply wants it, the person will sacrifice almost anything to get it. At the very least, the person will rationalize until convinced that the only proper course of action is to purchase the product.

Hmm! Nice Car!

Think about the last time you absolutely had to have something like a new car. Remember the car you used to drive? You loved that car. It worked well for you. It still looked good, was comfortable, and had all of your stuff carefully and conveniently stowed exactly where you could get to it. In moments of contentment, you may have even mumbled to yourself, "I'm never going to get rid of this car."

Then, the inevitable happens. Abruptly, and without notice or warning, you see a new car you like. Nothing intentional, mind you — not flirtatious or lustful — just an innocent passing thought. ("Hmm! Nice car! I'd look good in that.") From that moment, your current car becomes "that old clunker that is a constant embarrassment to me and my family" and "that car is on its last leg." You may deny that you really want or have any intention of buying a new car (that lovely, sleek, glowing, engineering masterpiece). After all, you were just being observant. Wrong. You're gone, Charlie. It is too late. Your current car is not long for your garage.

You'll continue to think of millions upon millions of reasons why you need that car. Not want, not desire, not crave, or even covet — you NEED it.

In this example, did you notice that not once did you tell yourself that you couldn't afford the car. Finances have nothing to do with this purchase. You reserve the "I can't afford it" phrase for your negotiation process with the dealer on the day you purchase. Incidentally, it won't bother the dealer too much either. Smart salespeople have read my book, too. This dealer knows what your "I can't afford it" really means.

Even as you stand before the dealer, your mind is jumbled. It races with thoughts. ("I've seen your ad. I've seen your car. I have appeared in front of you at my own volition. I'm ready. I'm yours. Please make it possible for me to leave my clunker here and drive away with my image of what I can be in that new thing. And, please, please don't believe me when I say, 'I can't afford it.' All I ask is that you sell me the car, but be gentle with me.") At this point, you're probably willing to forego other purchases, maybe even necessities, to have that car.

Recognizing This Crucial Point

Once you recognize what customers or clients mean with the "I can't afford it" statement, you can focus attention on finding and filling the prospect's true wants and needs versus pressuring that person to buy. Remember that only the prospect's perception matters.

Customers will buy what they want, not necessarily what you believe is good for them or what an objective analysis may reveal as beneficial to them. This is one of those rare instances where all the homework and research may fail to produce the desired results.

Since the buying decision is an emotional one, you may find some customers' reasons for buying or not buying completely surprising and sometimes irrational. As a Friendly Persuader, you must be able to separate customers' true needs from emotional needs. Focusing on what is important to customers gives them compelling reasons to buy from you.

Emphasize What the Buyer Wants

Separating true needs from emotional needs can be tricky, especially if you fail to allow your Nemesis time to confirm true desires. When you dominate the conversation, you will seldom learn what is important to clients. Once customers' desires are known, discuss ways your product supplies or fills that desire or need. At this point, discussing benefits would be useless.

Let's use Company A as an example. If Company A frequently mentions the need for fast service and you can provide fast service, emphasize that point by discussing in detail the steps you take to assure promptness. While it may be true that most of your other customers buy because you offer the largest variety of products or services, forget that spiel for the time being. Instead, stress the way you can satisfy Company A's need for speedy service. With this technique, you have given your customer a compelling reason to buy—fast service. Closing the transaction or making the sale should be a piece of cake.

Talking through the Close

Do you ever get a craving for an exotic food or a certain flavor or brand of ice cream? Most crave a special meal or treat occasionally. It's usually easy to satisfy that desire by picking the appropriate restaurant. Your customers are no different. When a particular reason for considering your product surfaces, that reason, whatever it may be, is what the customer wants to talk about.

For the same reason that a hamburger doesn't sound good when you want pizza, a lower price won't entice a client to buy when the dominant need is for reliable service. Since you must assume that only one or, at best, a few virtues of your product are likely to interest a particular customer, don't attempt to promote a smorgasbord when your Negotiating Nemesis desires a single item. Nothing else you may offer will be appetizing to him or her at this time, so you are wasting your efforts.

To avoid this fatal error, a Friendly Persuader keeps the customer talking in order to identify the true needs and desires of the customer. This talking on and on, called *talking through the close*, will eventually lead to a sale.

Some flawed marketing campaigns offer salespeople huge incentives to move outdated or unpopular products. Certainly, some customers can use these products, but if sales skyrocket, it's a matter of short-term commissions and bonuses outweighing most customers' true needs.

While the sales incentives allow for a clean warehouse, you may have transferred your junk to your customers' warehouses. When you overload customers with too many bargains, you risk losing regular business with them until the bargains are sold. Customers may also conclude that you sold them obsolete or inappropriate merchandise, a practice that can permanently cost you their business.

Compare how often businesses reward attempts to generate long-term customer goodwill with the number of times they reward people for merchandise clearance. To unload the inventory effectively and avoid angering a client, consider a specific action or offering. Perhaps you could insert a direct-mail piece or special-offer flier with the monthly invoice. Be honest and say you are marking it down because it's last year's model or it doesn't have the latest features.

Giving a reason for underselling at a very good price will pull in an immense response and will keep customers returning to you. Telling a sales staff to unload the old stuff or else the paychecks will be late invariably brings opposite results. A better approach is to have personnel *talk* through the close. When customers' needs are met, you turn "I can't afford it" into "Wrap it up. I'll take it home."

Value Deflates the "I Can't Afford It"

To defuse the "I can't afford it" syndrome many companies successfully compare their products to competitive products that are far more expensive or more capable. Though the comparison highlights various features and isn't a complete one-on-one comparison, simply noting that the much more expensive product has a similar feature elevates the prospective buyer's perception of a less expensive product's value.

For example, many car companies mention that their vehicles have features found on a BMW, a Mercedes, or a Rolls Royce. They never say their car is the same as or as good as the more expensive car, but merely mentioning even one shared feature makes the lower-priced car appear more valuable. Simply compare some aspect of your product or service to the recognized best in your industry, and *bingo,* you have instantly enhanced the perceived value of your product.

If your product is top-of-the-line, it is more than likely the most expensive. Don't be shy admitting it. Some people routinely buy from the most expensive suppliers, assuming that their products are the best, which isn't always true. If yours is the best and your customer needs the best, be ready to explain why and how the best suits the customer's needs. For example, reliability may be the customer's paramount concern. The best car is usually more reliable, so your power negotiating point is that your product will reduce the risk of breakdown and thereby minimize lost time or lost efficiency.

It Costs Nothing Unless You Can Use It

Another way to keep value in perspective is to routinely associate product benefits with cost. When you're asked, "How much?" (And, you will be asked, sometimes before the prospect even knows what the product is) you can follow these two rules:

➤ *Don't give a price early in the discussion if you can possibly avoid it.*

➤ *Always associate benefits with price.*

To abide by the first rule, the Friendly Persuader can deflate premature cost concerns by saying, "It won't cost anything unless you can use it." Another alternative is to break down the price into appropriate incremental units—the unit per day/per user/per application approach. You have heard the insurance sales pitch: "Only thirty-three cents per day gives you the protection you need." (Don't scoff, it's been working for years. Now you know why.) There's also the airline cost of seventy-five cents per passenger mile or expressing the cost of a deluxe stereo in your new car: "Only five cents per day for the time you will own this fine car." Or, we're all familiar with the recent "dime a minute" long distance phone service. You can express the cost of just about any product or service in terms of basic units. The result is that almost any item sounds inexpensive.

Include Benefits with Price

The second rule is easy to follow. Each time you quote a price, preface the dollar amount with the benefits. Instead of mentioning the costs of the seminar ($295) explain your price quote. "The full, two-day seminar, including all written materials, a live instructor who will be available to answer questions, and the take-home video lesson are yours for an investment of only $295." Such a benefit/quote combination produces visual images of value, which the prospect might otherwise fail to comprehend. Since the customer might not be able to imagine benefits, why take a chance?

From this point forward, the "I can't afford it" phrase will remind you that you failed to do your job and, worse still, that you didn't provide enough information for the customer to make an informed decision. Perhaps, you didn't give enough reasons to convince the buyer to purchase your product or service.

You need not apologize for making these mistakes. As a Friendly Persuader, you'll now be armed with the tools that allow you to counter a customer's or client's "I can't afford it" with an immediate "Of course you can. In fact, you can't afford not to have it. You see, I've saved the best for last. My product will...."

At this point, we separate the Friendly Persuaders from the panhandlers, the salespeople from the order-takers, the winners from the losers. Remember that the critical first step in the negotiating process is to plan and evaluate. You need to conduct research, perform self and product analysis, and ask questions.

A true Friendly Persuader will know customers' wants and needs and will make the Negotiating Nemesis want the product by diverting the discussion to how the product will benefit the customer. Remember that when someone says, "I can't afford it" that person is not talking about money.

17
Asking for It

Retail clerks routinely ask, "Shall I wrap it up for you?" and "How are you paying for this?" These questions provide useful information and enable clerks to make an assumptive close. They assume you want the merchandise, and the questions cement your commitment and bring closure to the sale. This drawing toward closure eliminates indecision on your part and enables the clerk to uncover and deal with any remaining objections. Once the clerk eliminates objections, the impetus of the pending close shifts to the customer. If no sale occurs, the clerk is free from fault.

When faced with such questions, what is your next move? You could ignore the clerk or pretend to have fallen into a trance and stare into space or silently slither away. Of course, you will do neither. Unless the clerk had a poor sense of timing, you will respond because you are ready to wrap up your negotiations. Since you always attempt to maintain control, you will take the initiative and shift from the negotiating stage to finalizing the sale. When clerks move toward closure, customers generally wind up amid one of the most effective closing techniques, making choices. When offered choices, customers must choose. In a retail purchase, you choose between "cash or charge?" With a major consumer item such as a car, the dealer may asks if you prefer "red or green." In a multimillion dollar real estate transaction, the agent may inquire "twenty year or twenty-five year financing?"

People prefer making selections because choosing grants them a feeling of control. Notice that I said they have a *feeling* of control. They may or may not *be* in control, but they will feel as if they are. A good illustration of this principal can be found at the checkout counter of your supermarket. How many times have you heard the "paper or plastic" question? That's right. Every time you have passed through the line, you've heard it. What is the answer everyone gives? The inevitable answer will be either "paper" or "plastic." You have never, ever heard anyone respond with "Hmmm. Let me see. Do you have any of those little cloth bags with cute little handles?" No. The response is always "paper" or "plastic." Two choices always elicit an answer.

The customer gives the answer and feels good about it, but who really has the power? The clerk does. Allowing the customer to feel this control is of utmost importance. A Friendly Persuader offers carefully selected choices. Regardless of which choice the Negotiating Nemesis selects, the Friendly Persuader wins because, in advance, the deck is loaded with two choices, both favorable to him or her.

Rely on the Experts

Another closing technique removes adversarial relationships and directs decision-making responsibilities onto more knowledgeable persons. If, for example, *Consumer Reports* acknowledges your product as the best buy in its category, or if reviews by recognized authorities in trade publications regard it as the best, refer prospective buyers to those sources.

Reviews from experts indirectly shift responsibility away from you and your customers. Since most feel more comfortable with written reports anyway, these reports turn buyers' insecurities, which stem from relying on dealers' or clerks' opinions, into positive reinforcements which move customers toward the closure of the sale.

Share Testimonials

You can further strengthen closings with testimonials from others (not necessarily experts) who have faced similar decisions. Customers validate personal opinions when they realize that others with a similar bent are satisfied with their product or service. Most pride themselves on their own perceived brilliance.

Alternatively you could share the unfortunate consequences of those who made bad choices. Insurance agents often share such stories with young couples who are hesitant to purchase life insurance. As a life insurance agent during college, I have a particular example I will share. A recent male college graduate (claiming to be "young and healthy" and knew he would "live a hundred years") was tragically killed in an auto accident the weekend after he turned down my sales pitch. For the next two years, I shared this shocking and tragic story with all young breadwinners who made similar comments.

Besides sharing testimonials or authoritative reports, be sure to review past deals that were successful for you and match similar situations with closing techniques that have previously worked. This combination increases your chance of closing a transaction. To assure success, carefully analyze techniques, picking only those which match positively your personality and that of your Nemesis.

Go for the Close

While it is great sport and certainly challenging and sometimes fun to negotiate what you or your company needs, unfortunately you fail to profit if, despite the intensity, you fail to reach a conclusion. In sales lingo, it's the *close* that counts. A similar close appears in the movie, *Jerry Maguire*, where we Friendly Persuaders find one of the best lines of all times: "Show me the money!"

You must recognize that negotiating efforts will go unrewarded until an agreement is attained. Avoid stalls and keep negotiations moving forward. You must know when to end the negotiations. You end precisely when a settlement has been reached. Why continue the process when you have agreed? Despite this knowledge, many foolishly insist on completing a planned presentation. Whether it's a ten-reasons-to-buy pitch or a detailed analysis of every aspect a prospective customer could consider, some of us become enamored with the presentation and lose sight of the primary objective.

Remember that few buy based on your extended list of reasons. Once customers receive enough benefits to validate personal opinions, they subconsciously shift their focus to satisfying personal wants and needs. Sure, it is tempting, even seductive, to continue with your brilliantly prepared dissertation. After all, you masterfully designed it, and since you exerted an enormous amount of time and energy into it, you feel compelled, even driven, to deliver it. You may feel that if you finish with anything less than the whole presentation, you neglect your obligation to your company or to yourself. Those less skilled in negotiations may allow egos to rise, leaving them with such thoughts as, "How dare the customer interrupt" even to say, "I'll take it!"

If you are clever, and I know you are, you will forget the brilliant sales pitch and negotiate to resolve remaining issues and make the sale. The presentations you orchestrated and slaved over are expendable and are well worth sacrificing in exchange for an agreement. You seek the agreement, so avoid ruining it by continuing to show how well you can deliver a designated volume of data.

Son, the Sale Is Done

I have a close friend, a sales professional, who always boasts, "I don't care who he is or where I am. When the man says, 'Yes,' I close my book and leave. Son, the sale is done." He's been repeating this corny singsong for years now while earning well into a six-figure income.

While this line may be corny, it underscores that the key element in the negotiation process is the agreement and not the interaction with a client. When facing an early agreement in a negotiation, it is natural to feel frustrated when cut short of delivering the full load of

data. Since your Negotiating Nemesis will also have
preparations curtailed, he or she, faces similar tension.
If you pressure your Nemesis with your idea of the best
solution, even if it is the most logical solution, your
Nemesis will seldom be receptive unless granted equal
time to share ideas.

When in Doubt, Listen

Convincing your Negotiating Nemesis to accept
your solution should be your primary goal, yet once
that goal is met, you must end your presentations and
allow your Negotiating Nemesis a chance to share any
remaining concerns. When you are unable to ascertain
your Nemesis' next ploy, you must again move from
talking to listening. Remember that if your Negotiating
Nemesis keeps asking for oranges, stop increasing your
discount on apples and switch to oranges.

Look for Shortcuts

If negotiations stall or drag on, search for shortcuts.
To increase your rate of success in negotiations and
save valuable time, quickly unearth your Nemesis'
wishes or needs. Without discovering those needs,
there is little way to adequately prepare any
presentation since you will most likely waste time
concentrating on the wrong issue.

Consider what would happen if a car salesperson
failed to recognize that a potential customer had
abandoned a broken-down junker one block away and
literally walked onto the lot. If the salesperson
aggressively boasts of accessories or color choices the
customer could custom order and receive packaged

with the car next month, the customer, with no car to drive, will rapidly lose interest. This customer has one primary concern — the immediate purchase of a car. The salesperson could sell a purple polka dot car with no radio if it were the only car available. This man is walking.

Avoid making the tragic mistake of assuming that your Negotiating Nemesis sees merit in what you place value upon. Exhume this flawed thinking and realize that others have different needs and wishes and identify those as early as possible.

So, when the retail clerk asks, "Shall I wrap it for you?" you should wrap up your negotiations and take the initiative to shift from negotiating to a final settlement.

Timing

When finalizing negotiations, keep timing in perspective. When do you close? Do you wait until your Negotiating Nemesis suggests closure? Of course, experience is the best teacher, and with skill, your intuitive perception will guide you toward the correct decision. While you build your negotiating skills, my three-step negotiation model — prepare, ask, and *trade-off*— will help you decide when to conclude.

Just as the retail clerk poses a closing question to discover how you will pay for purchases, you can resolve minute issues in your own closing questions. If you avert closing until all possible queries are resolved, you may symbolically end up on a train that never stops. Instead, it just keeps rolling down the track forever. As you close, minor issues will vaporize, and you will discover that some seemingly more important ones were disfigured objections your opponent used as a delay tactic and cast them in the mix just to avoid making a commitment. Price objections frequently fit into this category. Closing will separate the real from the imaginary and allow the true unresolved issues to surface where they can be properly addressed and the negotiation nullified. Here, then, are the key elements of timing:

> *First, prepare by having data available that allow you to determine what the other person wants and needs. Although this information-gathering step actually continues throughout the negotiation, you should be thoroughly prepared before you begin.*

> *Next, ask for everything you want, stating all items in terms of how they benefit the other person.*

> *Third, trade-off. As you ask, be willing to make concessions and modify, not necessarily reduce, your requests. Be certain to allow others ample time to voice concerns and wishes. When you're confident you have the data you need, have asked for what you want, and have traded concessions to resolve issues, stop negotiating. Yes, stop negotiating. It is not necessary to wait until you have resolved all possible issues to close. After closing, you can smooth out agreements on remaining items.*

18
Negotiating the Non-Negotiable

A noted politician once said, "Just because I said it, doesn't make it so." Always assume that your Negotiating Nemesis is an aspiring politician. Even when the unit price for goods or services is fixed, frozen, or given any other label that implies it's non-negotiable, don't give up and automatically assume that point to be true. How do you find out? Simple.

The Friendly Persuader does the unthinkable and *asks*. Ask for discounts. If you receive a price concession, offer to buy just to hear and see the response. Ask about free delivery or quantity pricing or floor samples or closeouts, anything at all. One good approach is to ask if discounts have previously been given. Simply raising the price issue puts your Nemesis on the defensive. Then, attentively wait for your Negotiating Nemesis to respond. When you're certain the final-and-lowest-price is at hand, whether your Nemesis has lowered the previously non-negotiable price or not, it's time to accept the price but request that something you value be tossed in as an incentive. If adequately prepared, you will ask for an item or service that costs the other party little, if anything. Nevertheless, it will have value to you or your firm.

Hidden Opportunities

As a Friendly Persuader, you will find that you are, almost daily, bombarded with opportunities to better your position, yet untrained negotiators are seldom cognizant of these breaks. Since most are obsessed with price, then price remains the most often discussed aspect of any transaction, (total price, unit cost, quantity discount, etc.). However, once a price has been established, both sides in the negotiation frequently tend to ignore pertinent details.

For analogy purposes, let's say that the price of an item you wish to purchase is fixed. Certainly, many products and services have a predetermined, often preprinted (published) price. All too frequently, people consider preprinted terms and conditions to be cast in stone. With such firm pricing, is there room to improve your deal? When dissected, many aspects of any sale are negotiable. To fully comprehend any deal, it is necessary to pull your eyes off price and concentrate on other areas where you can profit. Whether buying or selling, if you glance with new respect at the pages of any written material, you can improve your negotiation stance in almost any situation.

Your Price, My Terms

One possible area you can favorably negotiate is financing, a concept readily illustrated with a maxim borrowed from shrewd real estate investors: "Your price, my terms." Applying this concept to a specific transaction may lead to an offer such as, "I'll pay your $200,000 price with no payments for the first five years and then interest only for five more with amortized payments for twenty years." Admittedly, this example is extreme (although not impossible), but you get the idea. You don't have to be a financial wizard to conclude that the buyer gains a substantial advantage, if not a windfall, from the delayed payment schedule. The time value of the money more than offsets the paying of an excessive purchase price.

The 2.5 Million Dollar Deal

Let me illustrate this point. A few years ago, I had an opportunity to acquire a large fifty-acre undeveloped tract of land right in the heart of the hottest section of what promised to be a burgeoning resort community.   Speaking for the corporation that now owned most of my net worth, I was approached by a *local,* that is, a man who was there right after God, but before tourism.

This man's opening remarks expressed his desire to sell the land for $2.5 million, and he followed up this comment with a history of how he had purchased the land several years ago for $167,000 and always knew that someday it would be worth $2.5 million. Since he felt the land was now worth $2.5 million, he was prepared to sell.

In my opinion, he was only half right. Clearly, he was ready to sell, but the land was not yet worth $2.5 million. Although with the direction the boom area was taking, it would be worth that amount in a matter of months. At this point, we had only two elements established. He was a more-than-willing-seller, and the price was firmly set at $2.5 million.

Trying to keep a twinkle from my eyes as I stood beside him, I replied that if conditions were favorable,

I could be mildly interested in purchasing his land. First, I related that fifty acres was really more than I needed, reminding him that I was looking for a project location that would require several acres but not fifty. At no time did I mention that minimally I required only four to five acres, nor did I hint that his property was perfectly positioned for my project, which would in turn enhance the value of the remaining acreage.   In spite of my nonchalant attitude, as you've probably guessed, I was excited over his proposal but quietly contained my interest.   In response to my stated reservations, the owner pointed out that I could carve out the land needed for my project, hold the balance, and make a nice profit. *"Don't fling me in that briar patch!"*

Explaining that I had only $300,000 available for the land purchase and that I was unaware of financing possibilities on a $2.5 million acquisition, I astutely highlighted the fact that not only was I from another state which automatically made real estate financing difficult but there was another problem.   Considering the relatively small size of the local financial institutions and the large expanding district, my prospects of obtaining a large amount of money to invest in his land were poor.   (Can you picture Huck Finn and the picket fence?)   Eager to make the deal, my Negotiating Nemesis countered that he didn't need all the money right away, for tax reasons, and that he would happily "carry the paper" for me and "earn a little interest."

Amazingly, the seller took control of outlining the deal.   It seems he had bought and sold a lot of land in the area and was quite familiar with how to prepare the transaction.   He had an attorney who practiced close by who could draw up the transaction and a friend at the local title company who could conclude the deal.

My company acquired the fifty-acre tract for $2.5 million. I gave him my $300,000 and a promissory note for $2.2 million secured by a deed of trust. At closing, my company received a release deed giving us clear title to the parcel of land we first needed but instead of a four or five acre release, we had him release seventeen acres. With seventeen acres free and clear and another thirty-three acres secured by a first trust deed note for $2.2 million and interest set at eight percent per annum, we were in business. Payment terms consisted of interest only for eight years, payable quarterly. The seller also included a provision that stipulated that any missed quarterly interest payment would simply be added to the note as principal.

I was sitting pretty! My plan to buy four or five acres for $300,000 turned into fifty prime acres, seventeen acres immediately free and clear and another thirty-three acres that could continue to grow with the boom. As the land rapidly increased in value, I could, if I chose, avoid paying even one cent more for eight years. Of course, the contract further included release clauses allowing us to sell parcels of the land from time to time. Why and how did I get such a great deal? The seller, obsessed with price, was not particularly interested in anything else. I paid him his price; I got everything else.

Where the Money Meets the Sea

Another instance of financing as a negotiating factor occurred when I lived in Rancho Santa Fe, California, for five years. As Danny Santucci, the lawyer/comic (Yes, Virginia, there is such an animal) would say, "That is where the money meets the sea!" Mind you, at the time, I could not rationally afford to live there, but I am a good negotiator—a Friendly Persuader.

A real-estate agent and investor I knew once asked for my advice. She had met an elderly gentleman who had the perfect house for her to purchase. It was a two-bedroom cottage with five acres of gently sloping land overlooking a twenty-acre lemon grove. He had told her that she could move in now and after the upcoming marriage, she and her contractor husband-to-be could sell the house and make a very nice profit.

She explained it this way. "He wants $1 million for the house, which is about $100,000 over-priced," my friend Wendy reported. "It's absolutely perfect for me. He will carry the financing with only $50,000 down. I can swing that. The problem is that even with great terms and the small down payment, I would still be overpaying. What's the solution?"

"I assume, by the small down payment and owner financing, that he does not need the money," I responded.

"No, he doesn't, but he's very firm on his price. In fact, you might say he's stuck on it—won't budge a penny," Wendy complained.

"If he wants his inflated price and is willing to finance, don't pay him any interest," I suggested.

While highly unorthodox, such an arrangement is legal. Yes, for tax purposes, the IRS will take a principal-only-payment loan and figure it as if it included interest, calling it assumed interest. Yet, that's the IRS. As long as capital gains tax rates are just about the same as the ordinary income tax rate, it makes little, if any, difference.

A promissory note is a negotiated agreement

between two parties who can agree to any rate of reasonable interest. Some states' usury laws are strong enough to force the lender to forfeit the debt if excessive interest is charged. Knowing the offer was unusual, Wendy asked how she could pose such a bid. I first suggested that she discuss the offer with the buyer and specifically find out how much time he would allow on the term of the note. (She expected him to offer ten years, which was satisfactory with her.) Once he commits to terms, she should explain that she had hoped for a longer term, saying, "But if I give you your price and give you your term, I can't afford to give you any interest."

Mind you, folks, before making such an offer, you'd better practice it in front of a mirror to avoid breaking out laughing in the middle of the presentation or fainting when it's accepted.

Wendy presented the offer, and the buyer agreed. I wasn't shocked, but I was a little surprised. I had expected a 3% to 5% interest counter-offer from him. Given the discounted cash flow value and term length of the note, she'd saved well in excess of the $100,000 that she had initially wanted to trim from the price.

Accept a Good Deal

Years ago, when I taught real estate investors how to negotiate, I frequently used the zero-interest ploy for shock value, attempting to make the point that so many terms and conditions often assumed to be non-negotiable are negotiable. These sessions ended with a challenge: "If you can get anyone to agree to that, write me, and I'll buy you a trophy." Before long, I discontinued making this statement because the trophy costs started eating into my annual income.

Before her deal closed, Wendy told me that she desperately wanted to know why the seller so readily accepted her offer. She had to ask. *Remember, Dear Readers, and this is important. Get a pencil and write this down: accepting a good deal is usually better than dissecting it.* I warned Wendy not to open that can of worms until after the transaction was closed. She couldn't wait, so she asked.

Here's the answer: "Of course, I know about interest, and I know what a good deal I gave you, but I'm very rich and have no one to give the house to, except a vulture of a nephew who deserves nothing. Besides, I made a bet with the guys I play cards with at the Country Club that I could get a million dollars for my cottage and sell it within the month at that price. I had over-bragged, but it made me mad that they teased me so much. I bet them a bottle of Crown Royale that I could do it, and that bottle on the cupboard is my prize."

The lesson learned is to never attempt to think for your Negotiating Nemesis. Study the person as well as possible, but don't make decisions for them.

Other Negotiation Factors

Other factors that may be negotiable when price is fixed include delivery, installation, and training. If you sell goods or equipment, the cost of delivery, installation, setup, and all the other services necessary to make a product functional can be significant. Some companies, even entire industries, have standard ways to allocate shipping costs. When you compare quotes or offers from different companies, be sure all parties treat shipping the same way. Don't assume shipping charges are non-negotiable.

Besides shipping, which is sometimes treated as a part of the purchase price, find out who has the authority to handle or switch payments for additional services and negotiate that payment in your favor. Although their accounting systems differ, many companies account for the cost of installation, setup, and training from a budget center other than the sales department.

By allocating these costs to a different department, the amount spent on training or the setup may not concern the salesperson. An example is a car salesperson promising a buyer free service for the first year. The salesperson sells the car. The service manager then has to worry about the service department's profitability. Why not ask for the arrangement when you buy your next car? Be sure to get the agreement in writing to avoid potential misunderstandings.

As a Friendly Persuader, you have gathered information about how your buyer or seller accounts for delivery, training, and setup as you plan your negotiation strategy. You'll be ready to ask for many items of value that cost your Negotiating Nemesis nothing. Generally, you'll find these no-cost-to-them items are easy to obtain.

Soft-Dollar Concessions

When trading benefits at any phase of the negotiation, it's usually easier to get soft-dollar concessions than hard-dollar concessions. Hard dollars, here, mean cash dollars while soft dollars represents items of value that don't require payment to or from your

Negotiating Nemesis.

Suppose that as a concession I asked you to give me 500 free copies of your next book. If it were a publishing-house book, you, as the author, would have to pay nearly the full retail price for each book. The top discount is often only 40% off the retail price and many stores offer discounts almost that high.

On the other hand, suppose I asked you to mention me in your next book. That would cost you nothing, but the value of your recommendation could bring in a potential windfall in new business.

Just as it's generally easier to win concessions on soft-dollar items than on hard-dollar items, you should avoid excluding the possibility of a hard-dollar concession unless you're receiving either a very important soft-dollar item or an equal or better hard-dollar value. Confusion can occur in the heat of the negotiation process, but the Friendly Persuader keeps the hard and soft-dollar distinctions clearly in focus and easily pulls them forward as needed.

Some products or services can be customized for your business at a relatively small or insignificant cost to suppliers. This extra touch, such as stamping your company label on a product or offering extra color choices for consumer products, adds value that often translates to dollars in the marketplace. Tapping into this potential source of profit can result in your ultimately receiving more benefits than if you had haggled over price and received a small concession.

I remember once seeing a jet filled with executives taxi into the corporate jet terminal of an airport to drop off VIP's for a meeting with key customers' corporate leaders. When the plane parked, the company name was prominently visible on the side of the jet.

After the limos departed to deliver the VIP's to their meeting, I spoke with a crew member who admitted to me that the jet was chartered for the occasion. Placing a client's logo on the plane was a service the charter company gladly offered. The cost to the company that chartered the jet was small compared to the benefits it sought — the powerful impact of appearing to be a company that owned a multimillion dollar jet.

Customize the Deal

To get a large health maintenance organization's (HMO) business, a pharmaceutical company agreed to repackage their pills for the HMO in more convenient, smaller containers according to the HMO's specifications. Customizing made the deal work.

Another option is to restructure. This concept works well when you're told, "It's not in the budget." Companies do have departmental budgets and executives routinely spend all funds, yet if the company needs your products or services, the company managers will pull funds from a related budget account.

Suppose a company desperately needs to train maintenance personnel to service new machines but lacks money in the training budget. If your company provides the training, how can you meet the client's needs (and make your sale)? Suggest the client pay for the services from a different account and propose that perhaps there are available funds in the maintenance account.

My company has used this approach to provide live training, supplemented by video and workbooks, when customers had no training materials budget available. Our solution was to give away the materials free and charge the customer appropriately for the live instruction. Interestingly enough, we can offer the same training when an instructional budget is depleted but a materials budget is solvent. We give away the instruction and sell the material. See how clever and creative we are? Brain surgery, right?

Don't be concerned if a company places your services or goods in different categories than you placed them. Perhaps that is a way to distract funds to pay for items or services. When you let artificial limitations interfere with your meeting your customers' needs, you lose business.

The reverse is often also true. You may have to help customers around the well-intentioned, but shortsighted, organizational limitations. This approach works particularly well when working with large organizations, institutions, and government agencies.

A fixed price, list price, or standard contract — it makes no difference. Always negotiate. There's always something you can and should ask to receive.

19
The Ethics of Negotiation

"Watch your thoughts; they become words. Watch your words; they become actions. Watch your actions; they become habits. Watch your habits; they become character. Watch your character; it becomes your destiny." When Frank Outlaw made this admonition years ago, he must have had the Ethics of Negotiation in mind.

Contrary to popular opinion, the concept of ethics and successful negotiations are *not* mutually exclusive. Many people believe that the really successful negotiators are without ethics or concern for others. Quite the reverse is true. Those who negotiate without regard for others use a win-lose approach; one person "beats" the other in a contest of negotiating power. This technique, if effective at all, works only once or twice. After being beaten up, people stop dealing with such a negotiator. As losers share experiences with others, word spreads throughout the kingdom until, as it is said, the rest is history. Your reputation and credibility remain with you for the long term. These are important attributes to the foundation of your Friendly

Persuader negotiating character—too important to
throw away by attempting to gain a quick, unfair
advantage at every turn.

The Home Run

A properly equipped and trained Friendly Persuader
is able to consistently receive what is desired in exchange
for what can be given up. And, the Friendly Persuader
is able to do so in an "everybody wins" environment,
rather than a win-lose, one-time, slam-bang, gotta-
have-it-all shutout. There are far more positives to the
"everybody wins" approach than there are negatives.
It's even possible for a Friendly Persuader, who has
properly planned a careful approach to an impending
negotiation, to find that his or her Negotiating Nemesis
is also inclined toward an "everybody wins" approach.
In baseball, this is known as a home run.

Ethical Guidelines

Since ethics are not only necessary in negotiations
but are also beneficial for both sides, it's important to
define guidelines. Let's start with two vital questions.
When should you negotiate? How far should you go?

First, you must not hesitate to continue to negotiate
even after an initial arrangement is relatively firm. This
doesn't mean you go back on your word. You simply
make sure everyone precisely understands and is in full
agreement with every minute detail of the negotiation
terms. Buyers are obliged to receive what they were
promised in every deal or transaction. Pointing out
deficiencies and requesting a remedy maintains the
integrity of the deal. Monitoring what you receive is

more than good management. It allows the person or people you're dealing with to correct any possible shortcomings.

Good Managers Appreciate Comments

As a customer, you can help save a business by calling attention to oversights or poor quality. Good business management appreciates your doing this service for them. You receive what you want, and the company stays in business. Who else is going to point out poor service? Certainly not competitors. If all dissatisfied customers only complained among themselves, the result would be that other potential customers would hear about it and be driven away. Eventually the business would fail. Believe me, good management will appreciate your comments. If your constructive service complaint is poorly received, you have positive proof of poor management, and with poor management, the business is going to fail sooner or later anyway.   Go ahead and begin looking for a new place to shop.

Competition Is Intense

Examples are everywhere. The restaurant business is a classic example of intense competition. If word gets out about less than adequate service or poor quality, the restaurant will soon be out of business.

While dining one evening at a favorite Italian restaurant, I watched in frustration as a waitress served our order to a nearby table and hustled away. The hungry and unsuspecting diners who received our order were confused for a minute or two as they sampled their meals and then realized what had happened. They soon had their *real order*, and the waitress discarded the mistake. Unfortunately, that meant our order had to start over, which translated to another 45-minute delay.

Considering the oversight understandable, but unacceptable, I intended to discuss it with a manager after dinner. I never received the chance. Illustrating how knowledgeable and effective managers work, this restaurant manager came to our table, apologized for the delay, and said he had already reduced our check by fifty percent. Although I wasn't looking for a delay or a discounted meal, his actions compensated for the inconvenience and insured our continued patronage of that restaurant. Less efficient managers would have waited for a complaint that may never have come.

Rather than putting up with poor products or service and maligning the business, you have an obligation to negotiate for what you deserve and keep good businesses in business.

How Much?

How much do you ask for? There's no right or wrong answer. You must determine this for yourself on a situation by situation basis. If business conditions favor you, you can demand (and receive) enough to win a short-term victory. Yet, if your demands end up putting your supplier out of business, how successful have you really been? Too much of that kind of success can ultimately cost you more or force your business to go under. Putting suppliers under duress to save a few extra dollars may cost you more later. There are plenty of stories of shortsighted suppliers negotiating windfall profits in times of raw material shortages. After the shortage, however, major contracts were switched from those greedy negotiators to suppliers who worked with customers.

Make sure what you ask for is tempered by a long-term perspective. Economic climates change. Buyers' markets can become sellers' markets overnight. The materials you purchased yesterday at a bargain price may someday be so scarce that only the orders of good customers are filled. As insurance against such a downward economic adjustment, you should always try to be on as many good customer lists as possible.

I once heard a customer of a limousine service tell how he fought and fought for the lowest price possible. He spent hours and repeated trips to the limousine company to negotiate the best deal. From his description of the negotiations, I could tell the company was only marginally willing but did agreed to supply the limo. The vehicle in question was one of those new, fancy stretch models — very expensive. The owner probably decided some revenue was better than none. Only an hour before the limo was scheduled to arrive, the limousine service called regrettably informing the customer that the new fancy limo had been in an accident and would not be available. Was the limo really wrecked? Or, did the owner find a more lucrative booking?

A year or two in court and attorney fees ten times the limo rental fee would provide an answer. It's unlikely the victim will spend the time and money to find out. Sometimes a deal that sounds too good to be true is too good to be true. Both sides lose. In this case, renting a replacement limo from any company would cost the customer more money and hassle. And, the limousine service has an unhappy customer spreading *ill-will* instead of *good-will*. Don't ever fight for the last nickel in a deal.

Some people view pursuit of goals as an ethical question. They assume the more zealous you are, the less ethical you must be. Let's clarify how this concept really works. Being unethical is not a question of how hard you press the other side for benefits. Demands and pressure don't decide how good you are as a negotiator. Demanding less is not more ethical and demanding more is not less ethical.

It's a matter of brain, not brawn. The results depend on how smart—not how taught—you are as a negotiator. Planning and probing for the real needs of your Negotiating Nemesis will produce far better results for you and your opponent. Meeting needs, without being pushy, produces the best results. Throughout this book, I have been repeatedly telling you that you can *get more by giving more*. Now, I'm telling you that you should *know more to get more*. Force only irritates the other side.

You may be asking, "Is there anything that is unethical?" Yes. Of course there are limits. While it's not necessary to reveal every aspect of your situation, it's not okay to lie or cheat. Just as dealing from the bottom of the deck is cheating in a card game, it's unprofessional and unethical to misrepresent what you can deliver. Hint that you may have a better deal over the horizon if you wish, but it's unethical to state something that is untrue. In all your negotiations, never offer what you cannot produce. It will cost you the game. Focus on benefits instead of forcefulness, and you and the other party will win.

Winners and Losers

It's easy to talk about avoiding win-lose opportunities

262 THE NEGOTIATING PARADOX

but much more difficult to actually practice. Is it generally because of greed? Is it because we have weak values? No. Actually, it's due to our prior conditioning. We grow up seeing that someone has to win and someone has to lose. Look at sports. Don't you go to a ball game to see who wins and who loses? There's even a scoreboard that constantly keeps us up on who's winning and losing. This competition is what makes it a sport.

Did you ever hear of a game where the teams compromised or agreed the score would be equal? Where would the sport be? One coach would merely contact the opposing coach on the morning of the game and perhaps over a cup of coffee negotiate the outcome. As a part of the negotiation, one of the coaches could contact the press and report the final score. The coaches could then meet at the golf course for a relaxing, post-game round. This wouldn't be sport. It would be absurd.

In most cultures and civilizations, there are winners and losers. We expect this scenario, so it's no wonder untrained negotiators try to win at all cost.

That's why some executives refer to their customers as the opposition. Negotiation is not a ball game; it's a relationship. If a relationship is to endure, it must be beneficial to all concerned. That's truly an everybody wins solution.

If a relationship is to benefit all concerned, the win-lose philosophy doesn't work. Marriage has been described as an ongoing series of negotiations. Have you ever heard of a successful marriage where the partners kept score?

Violating these principles is a common mistake in negotiation. Most negotiators focus their time and energy on what they want for themselves, viewing the negotiation process as a defensive activity. It's not. They're aiming at the wrong target. The successful Friendly Persuader aims first at the needs of the Negotiating Nemesis. To *meet* the needs of the other party, you must *know* the other party's needs. Then, you're equipped to employ your negotiating skills to fill as many of those wants and needs as you're able and willing to fill in order to get what you want and have wanted all along.

Before you make or respond to an offer you must always remember to first ask questions and then listen to your Negotiating Nemesis. You'll be shooting at the right target in your hunt for the *Best Solution*.

And, always, always remember the *Negotiating Paradox*. You can *actually* get more by giving more.